The two innocents

are outstanding representatives of the generation of libertarian intellectuals that emerged in Quebec about 1950 and during the next decade brought about the change of atmosphere that culminated in the Quiet Revolution.

JACQUES HÉBERT (born 1923) has written four travel books besides this one; a book of short stories; four books criticizing the judicial and penal system — one of them, *Trois jours en prison*, recording a first-hand experience during the long process for contempt of court and criminal libel that he endured as a result of his books challenging the court decision in the famous Coffin murder case; and a novel, *Les Écœurants*, which has been published in English as *The Temple on the River*. He has also edited *Ah! mes aïeux!*, an anthology drawn from the French-language press of 1867. He founded a weekly paper, *Vrai*, in 1954, and two book-publishing houses, Éditions de l'Homme in 1958, and Éditions du Jour, which he still heads, in 1961.

THE RIGHT HON. PIERRE TRUDEAU (born 1919) studied at the University of Montreal, the Harvard Law School, the Sorbonne, and the London School of Economics. During the 1950s he practised as a labour lawyer and was co-publisher and co-editor of the influential political magazine *Cité Libre*. For the first half of the 1960s he held the chair in constitutional law at the University of Montreal, until he was elected to Parliament as a nominee of the ruling Liberal Party in November 1965. He started this new career as parliamentary assistant to the Prime Minister, and entered the cabinet as Minister of Justice in April ˉ he succeeded the Right Hon. L. B. Pears and Prime Minister, and in the election led his government to the first parlia obtained by any party since 1957.

Jacques Hébert &
Pierre Elliott Trudeau

TWO INNOCENTS
IN RED CHINA

Translated by I. M. Owen

Toronto / New York / London

OXFORD UNIVERSITY PRESS

1968

Printed in Canada by
MC CORQUODALE & BLADES PRINTERS LIMITED

Contents

Illustrations

A note on this edition

The publication of this book in translation eight years after the journey it describes gives rise to some misgivings. In the meantime the condition of its subject and of at least one of its authors has changed considerably. In judging its contents I must ask the reader to keep two factors constantly in mind. For all I know, many of the observations about China (and more than a few of the statistics) may now be out of date. Some of the passing references to Canada, such as to the restrictive policy of the Quebec Censorship Board, are certainly no longer valid.

This book was not written by the Prime Minister of Canada, or by any public official, but by two private citizens responsible only to themselves for inaccuracies or indiscretions.

As I have had some experience of a private critic's unguarded words being used, years later, against a public figure, I add an all-purpose disclaimer. If there are any statements in the book which can be used to prove that the authors are agents of the international Communist conspiracy, or alternatively fascist exploiters of the working classes, I am sure that my co-author, Jacques Hébert, who remains a private citizen, will be willing to accept entire responsibility for them.

There is at least one comment in the book which I believe to be as true today as it was when we left for Peking: '. . . it seemed to us imperative that the citizens of our democracy should know more about China.' Perhaps that is why I am not entirely dismayed that this frank and informal treatment of a controversial subject should belatedly receive a new lease on life.

PIERRE ELLIOTT TRUDEAU

Ottawa, August 1968

Translator's note

Most English-Canadian readers will require, as I did, one explanatory note. Charles-Paschal-Télésphore Chiniquy (p. 1) was a priest who first became famous in 1844 as a temperance crusader, was involved in two scandals that led to his excommunication, was ordained as a Presbyterian minister at the age of fifty, and wrote a series of sensational anti-Catholic books which were at one time known around the world.

Two other references will be familiar to Canadian readers but not to others. Henri Bourassa (p. 67), Quebec nationalist leader and founder of the Montreal newspaper *Le Devoir*, was noted for his oratory; and at a Eucharistic Congress in Montreal he made an extemporary speech, in reply to the suggestion that French Canadians ought to speak English, which was published under the title *Religion, langue, nationalité* (1910).

'Frère Untel' (p. 82) is the pseudonym of Brother Pierre Jérôme (Jean-Paul Desbiens), whose biting critique of Quebec education and society, *Les Insolences du Frère Untel*, was published by Jacques Hébert in the year of the events recorded here. It was this book that popularized the term '*joual*' (allegedly a rural pronunciation of *cheval*), which had been introduced by André Laurendeau, editor of *Le Devoir*, as an epithet for the kind of slovenly French that he wanted to banish from Quebec speech.

Finally, alert readers will notice that there were five members of the group that included Messrs Hébert and Trudeau, and will find it hard to establish a list. For the record, the other three were: Denis Lazure, psychiatrist; Micheline Legendre, puppeteer; and Madeleine Parent, trade-union official.

I.M.O.

Preamble

This book was nearly given a different title: *The Yellow Peril: New Edition, Revised, Corrected, and Considerably Enlarged by Jacques Hébert and Pierre E. Trudeau*. This would have recalled to more than one reader the picture of China preserved in his subconscious: a land swarming with a multitude of little yellow men, famished, crafty, and (more often than they had any right to be) sinister.

Among all the terrors with which paranoiac educators sought to blight our childhood — freemasonry, the Protocols of the Elders of Zion, Bolshevism, American materialism, the Red Heel, Chiniquy, and what else? — the Yellow Peril occupied a prominent place.

As schoolboys, we learned from missionary propaganda that China was the natural home of all scourges: pagan religions, plagues, floods, famines, and ferocious beasts. The periodic collection taken up for 'stamps of the Holy Childhood' was also an opportunity to remind us of the wretched and slightly devilish state of a people who threw their babies to the pigs. And adventure tales featuring pirates of the China Sea or Fu Man Chus of the Shanghai underworld completed the education of our young minds in the dangers that lurked in the Dragon Empire.

It was during our adolescence that the Peril took on definite shape. College professors soberly proved to us, with statistics, that the demographic surge would soon burst the bounds of China and engulf the white world in a yellow tidal wave. About this time Mr 'Believe-It-or-Not' Ripley was diffusing another arresting image: if the Chinese people marched past a given point in fours, the parade (taking account of the birth- and death-rates) would continue throughout eternity!

We don't know if these images are still current today, or if children still advise each other not to breathe the tainted air if they pass an Oriental in the street. But we are compelled to remark that the adult world around us is unconsciously inspired by the same phantasms, all the more now that the Yellow Peril flies the red flag of Bolshevism. Under the influence of this dual fear, our conduct is doubly irrational: in politics we refuse to recognize the existence of those who rule a quarter — soon to be a third — of the human race, and we don't deign to sit with them in the councils of the nations; in economics we hesitate to increase our trading relations with the most formidable reservoir of consumption and production that has ever existed; in spiritual matters we are perpetuating the established identification between Christianity and the most reactionary interests of the West, notably in linking the future of a certain kind of missionary effort to the (unimaginable) return to power of Chiang Kai-shek.

That China is still an object of fear is betrayed even in everyday conversation. Before our departure, people seriously told us: 'You are courageous to go over there!' At first we thought this was mockery, directed against frivolous travellers by those who were courageously keeping their noses to the grindstone. But no; other expressions used taught us what daring we were apparently displaying: 'Have you made your will? Accidents happen so quickly.' 'It is easier to go behind the iron curtain than to come out again.' 'Aren't you afraid of being held as hostages?'

In all humility we couldn't bring ourselves to take these stories seriously. Besides, we each had in our possession a document belonging to the Canadian government, in which the Secretary of State for External Affairs of Canada requested under his seal and 'in the name of Her Majesty the Queen' that the authorities of 'all countries' should 'allow the bearer to pass freely without let or hindrance' and should 'afford the bearer such assistance and protection as may be necessary'. Armed with such a precious safe-conduct, we didn't see why we should be bothered at presenting ourselves at the border of any country at all. Besides, as the ensuing history is going to show, the Chinese took infinite precautions to ensure our return home safe and sound. They seemed to be afraid that, if one of us chanced to drown in the Grand Canal or idiotically fell off the Great Wall, a certain section of the Western press would draw dramatic conclusions about the danger of restoring diplomatic relations with a country where the life of a 'French-Canadian Catholic' was held so cheap.

In reality the only fear that we might possibly have thought reasonable was that of being denounced and vilified by compatriots on our return *ex partibus infidelium*. And it is a fact that out of a hundred French Canadians invited to go on this trip the previous spring (true, this was before the fall of the Union Nationale government), fewer than twenty dared to answer, and more than half of them refused.

But it must be said that on this score the authors of the present volume were pretty well immune to reprisals by this time. Since both of them had been generously reproved, knocked off, and abolished in the integralist and reactionary press in consequence of earlier journeys behind the iron curtain, the prospect of being assassinated yet again on their return from China was hardly likely to impress them.

All in all, we two, who had never travelled together before but between us had been four times round the world, sailed nearly all the seas, explored five continents extensively, and visited every country of the earth except Portugal, Rumania, and Paraguay, discovered that we entertained the same outlandish philosophy of travel: we believed that those who have toured a country observantly and in good faith are in some danger of knowing more about it than those who haven't been there.

And it seemed to us imperative that the citizens of our democracy should know more about China. If when we were children the grown-ups had told us anything besides rubbish on this subject, and if they themselves had ever been encouraged to reflect that the unthinkable sufferings of the Chinese people deserved something more from the West than postage stamps, opium, and gunboats, China today might be a friendly country. And an important part of Western policy wouldn't have to be improvised in the back rooms of Washington and Rome on the basis of information gathered in Hong Kong and Tokyo by agencies that clip and collate various items from Chinese newspapers. So we thought some supplementary information, and an effort at comprehension, might be of some use.

It is true that, not speaking the innumerable Chinese dialects really fluently, we would be largely at the mercy (and it *was* a mercy!) of interpreters; that we would see only what the

authorities would let us see; and so on. But the same reservations apply to the testimony of Canadian tourists in Spain, Egypt,
or the Holy Land; yet nobody dreams of telling them that they
would talk more sense about these countries if, instead of going
there, they had kept their slippers on and stayed in Notre-Dame
de Ham-sud or Sainte-Emilienne de Boundary-line.

For what has been seen has unquestionably been seen; what
was translated was translated by a Chinese official interpreter, so
that it does at least tell us what he himself thinks. Besides, we
didn't lack points of comparison: the combined total of our
earlier sojourns in Asia came to nearly two years, partly spent
in pre-Communist China and partly in Taiwan.

We know that to some people the mere fact of going to
China and staying there at the expense of the Communists is
enough to vitiate any testimony. Such people clearly rate their
own and others' honesty dirt cheap.

There remain some individuals with the peculiar notion that
good faith towards China amounts to bad faith towards the non-
Communist world. To this argument we have no answer, except
that this is not the way we understand human nature. We
don't ask such people to read us or to believe us; and if they
still persist in denouncing us we ask them first to reflect on the
consequences of a purely negative anti-Communism.

For years anti-Communists of this kind have applied themselves to discrediting any evidence that might suggest that the
Russians were not stone-age barbarians. Then, suddenly, the
Soviets put gigantic Sputniks in orbit around the earth, photo-
graphed the other side of the moon, and confounded world
opinion with their scientific progress. It is evident, then, today
that Western governments would have done well to have listened
more carefully to travellers who told of the progress of the
USSR, and to have put rather less trust in the witch-hunters;
for since it was our policy to regard Communism as an enemy
or at least a rival, it would have been on the whole less dangerous to overestimate than to underestimate this enemy's intelligence.

It is partly to prevent the repetition of these errors with regard
to the Chinese People's Republic that the authors have written

the present work. Those who take seriously the precept 'Love thy neighbour as thyself' cannot object to our reporting such success as the Chinese government is having in leading its people out of several millennia of misery. For it is always our fellow-humans that progress of this sort benefits — whatever their political allegiance may be.

But there will still remain some readers to accuse us — according to whether they are fanatically pro- or anti-Communist — of having said too much that is bad or too much that is good about today's China. We accept this certificate of impartiality — and we nonsuit both parties. Let each of them console themselves with the thought that our testimony (if it is as biased as they will say) can only help to weaken their particular enemy by exaggerating his superiority!

And now, the journey begins.

1 In which the expedition nearly sinks in the Thames

A kingdom can have only one crown; if I do not dethrone my rival, he will dethrone me. — POPE INNOCENT III

LONDON. TUESDAY, 13 SEPTEMBER 1960

Montreal to London by jet. A dull passage: we didn't even get to use the life-rafts. And Hébert wasted five dollars on a flight-insurance premium.

Why London? Because no country in all the Americas recognizes Communist China, except (just lately) Cuba. A letter from Mr Chu Tu-nan, president of the Chinese People's Association for Cultural Relations with Foreign Countries, had notified us that our Chinese visas would be granted to us in London.

About five o'clock in the afternoon, then, we present ourselves at the office of the Chinese chargé d'affaires for this little formality. A young Chinese, all smiles and unction, admits us to the old house at 49 Portland Place. 'Mr Lin is waiting for you,' he says.

We, as it turns out, wait for Mr Lin — in a vast drawing-room that has known better days. Old furniture upholstered in green velvet, a large worn carpet: they haven't had occasion to throw a party hereabouts since the good old days of Chiang Kai-shek.

Mr Lin is late. The furniture is mildewing, the carpet is fraying — along with our patience. 'There's probably a plane leaving for Peking this very evening . . .'

We are exchanging criticisms on the immense Mao Tse-tung in technicolor enthroned above the fireplace, when a slender personage wearing a smile too big for him enters discreetly, on tiptoe: Lin himself!

Delighted to see us, of course. He runs from one to another, distributing friendly words, Chinese cigarettes, matches. We exchange commonplaces with the greatest possible conviction.

'You have been to China before?'

'No,' says Hébert. 'Hong Kong, Macao — they're not really China.'

But Trudeau went to China in 1949.

'*Really*?' says Mr Lin with lively interest.

'From Hong Kong I slipped into the territory still held by the Kuomintang. It was in a state of anarchy. I got myself as far as Shanghai while the Red Army was on the other side of the Yangtze. I would have liked to stay and watch the capture of the city, but a truce was proclaimed. It was not to last long, however; soon after I left, the Red Army entered Shanghai.'

'How amazing,' says Mr Lin, delighted. '*I* was in the Red Army at that time — in the very contingent that took Shanghai.'

'We might have met in 1949!'

The ice is broken. Mr Lin sends for tea, which he pours himself, remarking that it's certainly a small world. The excellent jasmine tea leads to confidences. We learn that Mr Lin has been in London for four years, that he studied English in Amsterdam — a lot of instructive facts like that. Not until the third cup do we get to the point of this friendly tea-party: the visas, and the tickets for China.

Mr Lin hands out the visa application forms. The usual questions, plus two that we have also been asked in Spain, Argentina, and a few Arab countries: 'Religion? Political party?' To the second question we long to answer 'Social Credit', just to see the reaction in Peking.

Mr Lin takes the forms and the passports. 'I'll be right back. Time to stamp the visas.'

On the table, near the teapot, are tickets from London to Peking. Bits of paper that will allow us to cross half the world and see China at last.

Mr Lin is taking his time in coming back. Let's just glance at these tickets: 'Departure 14 September, 0830 hours.' Hell! that's tomorrow morning.

What *is* Mr Lin doing? These Chinese! Still Orientals after all, never in a hurry, as we have always been taught.

Mao Tse-tung smiles down from his splendid gilt frame.

Mr Lin at last! He is smiling too. He has the passports. His smile seems rather forced.

'There is a small difficulty for three of you,' he says carefully, with the air of announcing to a group of invalids that they have small and unimportant cancers.

Mr Lin takes his courage in both hands. 'Look. In Miss Legendre's and Mr Hébert's passports there is a note from the Canadian Department of External Affairs that — that — '

He says no more, but we understand. In recent years, when the Department issues a passport, it sticks a leaflet on the last page full of careful advice to Canadian citizens travelling to Communist countries. In brief, these travellers are required, before departure, to notify the Canadian government of their plans and to indicate the probable length and the purpose of their journey — all of which we had done. Then, on arrival in a Communist country, they are required to report to the nearest Canadian or United Kingdom diplomatic or consular officer.

Why not? However, that's not what is bothering Mr Lin. The thing is that the Department of External Affairs of Canada has committed a terrible gaffe in the eyes of a Chinese official by using the term 'Mainland China'. The implication is that there is another China, an island one, that we call Formosa and the Chinese call Taiwan.

Micheline Legendre and Jacques Hébert suggest a way out: that Mr Lin should simply tear the questionable leaflet out of the passport, especially as it is held only by a mere spot of gum. Mr Lin's smile brightens: he must have foreseen this step, since the Chinese visas are already in the passports — except Trudeau's. 'The difficulty is more serious in Mr Trudeau's case,' says Mr Lin, no longer smiling. 'A little more tea?'

No, thank you. Three cups are quite enough.

There is drama in the air. 'A more serious difficulty?' inquires Trudeau (who already realizes the trouble).

'Yes. There is a Taiwan visa in your passport.'

'That's true, I went to Taiwan two years ago.'

'Hmm. What did you go to Taiwan to do?'

'I was travelling in that part of the world. Actually, I wanted to go to China, but your government hadn't given me permission. So I visited Japan, the Philippines — and Taiwan as it happened to be on my way. I had no sympathy for Chiang Kai-shek, but that was no reason for avoiding Taiwan.'

'I regret to tell you that the policy of my government is explicit on this point: we do not give a visa to anyone who has been to Taiwan.'

'But your government invited me to visit China.'

'Did my government know that you had been to Taiwan?'

'I don't suppose so. But what does it matter? I could have got a new passport before I left, and you wouldn't have known anything about my earlier travels.'

'True. But I do know now, and the regulation —'

'I could explain the matter to the Canadian High Commissioner's office here and get a completely new passport — possibly even today.'

'I am heartbroken,' says Mr Lin, really looking heartbroken. 'But my duty requires me to seek advice from Peking.'

We parley for over an hour, each of us invoking new arguments to convince Mr Lin that Trudeau is neither an agent of American imperialism nor an admirer of Chiang Kai-shek.

'Terribly sorry,' repeats Mr Lin, 'but I have to ask for authority from Peking before I give you a visa.'

There is no more point in insisting.

'In my telegram, however, I shall take your arguments into account. I will even add a word of recommendation.'

'How soon will you have an answer?'

'Let us have at least two or three days,' says Mr Lin, glancing at the five tickets spread out on the table like a mandarin's fan. The icy wind that was tempered just now by a little warm tea makes its way back into the great drawing-room. 'I could make a suggestion —' begins Mr Lin cautiously. He hesitates. 'A little more tea?'

No, really.

'Well. I suggest that Mr Trudeau should wait for the answer from Peking and that the others should leave tomorrow morning as planned.'

'And if the answer is negative?' asks Hébert.

'You will be in Peking in two days. There you will be able to put Mr Trudeau's case.'

We don't agree. The Chinese government ought to have informed itself sooner on the subject of Trudeau. 'They invited him; let them accept him, Taiwan visa or no Taiwan visa,' says Micheline Legendre categorically.

We decide to abandon the scheduled take-off and wait for the answer from Peking. In Montreal we had already elected Trudeau group leader — taking advantage of a meeting he wasn't at. The scene is becoming worthy of Corneille: 'We shall go with the Leader or we won't go at all!'

Mr Lin closes the fan and puts the five airline tickets back in his pocket. He seems annoyed with us, and we feel he has just learned something of the spirit of solidarity of the capitalists of the province of Quebec.

We leave him and go into the nearest pub; after all that tea a beer would be welcome.

Trudeau pays for the round: that'll teach him to go to Taiwan.

WEDNESDAY, 14 SEPTEMBER

London is a good town and Alec Guinness a wonderful actor; we see *Ross*, a play of Terence Rattigan's on the life of Lawrence of Arabia.

In the *Punch* that comes out today, a very amusing article about a traveller who has provided himself with two passports so as to go to China after visiting Taiwan. We thrust this timely article under Trudeau's nose; it begins, 'A touch of schizophrenia is useful if you want to visit the two Chinas, Nationalist and Communist . . .'

No news from Mr Lin.

THURSDAY, 15 SEPTEMBER

A meeting in Trudeau's room to decide whether we will go to Brecht's *The Life of Galileo* or Chekhov's *The Seagull*. We debate for a good while before the Leader announces casually, 'Mr Lin phoned —'

'Ah!'

'Peking has answered.'

'Ah!'

'I will have my visa in three hours.'

Three hours. Mr Lin is radiant. There is tea, and above all a magnificent album of photographs of China that he wants to show us. He turns the pages slowly, lovingly, as if it were a family album. Look, that's his grandmother! No, it's Madame Sun Yat-sen.

The flight is tomorrow night. We invite Mr Lin to go out to dinner with us. We shake hands.

The war will not take place; we have settled all that, we and Mr Lin.

2 London to Peking

Let observation with extensive view
Survey mankind, from China to Peru.

— SAMUEL JOHNSON

FRIDAY, 16 SEPTEMBER

London Airport. A BEA jet is waiting for us in the night, speckled with green, red, and white lights.

'Passengers for Moscow, please . . .' It's forty minutes after midnight.

This whole story seems so improbable.

SATURDAY, 17 SEPTEMBER

A few hours of sleep, coffee, and already Moscow is teeming below us.

The stopover lasts all day. Red Square, St Basil's, the Kremlin, the Bolshoi; we've 'done' Moscow.

At 11.45 p.m. we take our seats in an Aeroflot Tupolev-104.

SUNDAY, 18 SEPTEMBER

Three hours later, without meeting the least little U-2, we land at Omsk in the Urals. A forty-minute stop is announced, but we are delayed there for an hour and a half. The pilots and mechanics of Aeroflot are extremely prudent. It's a nuisance — but Russian planes don't crash. Some compensation.

Irkutsk, capital of Siberia. After an interminable stopover, we fly over Lake Baikal, crescent-shaped and embedded in high mountains.

With the Gobi Desert, glimpsed through a curtain of cloud (full of holes, luckily), we are over Mongolia — China already.

'Fasten your seat-belts!' Peking is below; immense, very grey, very near. The time? We no longer know how much we have gained since London. The TU-104 touches down on a modern landing strip — but on either side of the concrete, cabbages are planted. In the New China there isn't an inch of ground to spare.

As we leave the aircraft we see several groups of Chinese with their arms full of flowers, probably intended for the VIPs travelling with us: a Venezuelan senator, some leaders of the Indonesian Communist Party, a Burmese delegation, etc.

But there is a bunch of flowers for each of us: gladioli, red roses, and asters. It is Mr Wen, vice-president of the Cultural Association, who offers them to us, together with an equally touching bunch of flowers of rhetoric.

Our hosts seem as happy to welcome us to their country as we are to get there. How many kind words a Chinese interpreter has to know if he is to do this job properly! Ours — one English-speaking and one French-speaking — are almost excessively modest. They simply don't exist. If we ask them the time, they solemnly transmit our question to the vice-president, and give us his answer without even looking at their own watches.

No customs or police formalities; we are the guests of China. From the airport — larger and more modern than the Moscow one — we are driven to the Hotel Hsin Chiao, situated outside the walls of the old Chinese city, in the former 'concession' — the district where the European embassies huddled together behind high walls to keep out the rising tide of Asia.

Our friends of the Cultural Association, wishing to share our first meal with us, arrange to meet us at seven-thirty. Until then we have the freedom of the hotel, which, like all hotels in China, belongs to the State. It was built by the government five or six years ago. That's obvious: it is solid, functional, and drab.

The charms of Peking have been so vaunted in literature that there is some risk of disappointment at first glance. Everything is grey, no doubt because these grim walls have been battered for centuries by strong winds coming from the Gobi Desert, loaded with dust. The present régime has added nothing to the stern beauty of the imperial city, but it has made it into a modern capital, improving public services, multiplying large buildings, large squares, broad avenues — one of which, Tung Chang An Chieh, is a sort of compromise between Dorchester

Boulevard and the Champs-Elysées. Its name means 'Avenue of
the Long Peace', which does not prevent its use for great military
parades. It is there that we shall see, in two weeks, the extraordinary parade of October the First, the national day of the
New China. Here gather both the happy May Day crowds and
the 'spontaneous' demonstrations of protest against the imperialists.

On ordinary days, Tung Chang An Chieh reverts to being an
avenue of great peace indeed, where rare cars roll discreetly
along at twenty miles an hour; or pedicabs, also very rare,
struggle against the wind that blows all year round; or hurrying
pedestrians, out of their element, hasten towards more familiar
streets, built to their scale.

Seven-thirty. This hotel, intended for foreigners only, has two
dining-rooms. One offers European dishes (curried rice and beef
Stroganoff, for instance) and the other Chinese. Less from
politeness than by preference, it is in the latter that we have
arranged to meet our hosts.

Mr Wen is enchanted. He orders wine and beer: a rather
sweet red wine and a very light beer that reminds us of the
English beer we were drinking the day before yesterday in the
London pubs.

Mr Wen recites the menu: about ten dishes, which could not
be found together in Chinese restaurants anywhere else in the
world. The Chinese cuisine of Montreal, San Francisco, or Paris,
adapted to Occidental tastes, is vaguely like Cantonese cuisine.
But it has nothing to do with that of northern China.

We forage with our chopsticks in the plates of meat or fish,
drawing out of the depths of the sauce a huge shrimp, a wing of
duck, or — eating with chopsticks isn't learned in a day — a
modest mushroom.

Mr Wen answers our questions graciously, even humorously
if we insist. But it is quickly apparent that only one subject
interests him: the régime, its achievements, its projects. Perhaps
his propaganda is a bit ponderous, but isn't that better than
play-acting?

'This duck is simply delicious.'

'I can give you the recipe,' says Mr Wen with a laugh. 'That's not a state secret! In the old days, Chinese cooks guarded their culinary secrets jealously. Now there are no more secrets; their art is in the service of the whole people.'

Which doesn't mean that 650 million Chinese can afford lacquered duck every Sunday. But at the present rate of progress in China they are confident of being able to achieve it some day.

As he chatters on, Mr Wen tries to find out what interests us particularly, what we want to see in China. One of us wants to visit children's hospitals. Right. Another, to spend a day in a textile factory. Right. One is interested in marionettes. Naturally. Trudeau would like to talk law with some Chinese barristers. By all means. Hébert flatly demands to visit the Peking prison. Certainly, the day after tomorrow.

It's nine o'clock and bedtime comes early in China. In taking his leave, Mr Wen announces that during our stay in his country we will be able to count, twenty-four hours a day, on the solicitude of Mr Hou. In fact, this worthy Mr Hou, at once organizer of our travels, guide, official representative of our hosts of the Cultural Association, tireless guardian angel whom we call, in fun, the Commissar, was hardly ever to leave our sides for five weeks.

To watch over our comings and goings? To prevent us from meeting Chinese hostile to the régime? Who knows? But the other motives are so much more evident. The Chinese have a cult of hospitality which would be enough by itself to explain Mr Hou's solicitude. And then, the obsession that an accident might happen to a foreign visitor on Chinese soil. To avoid such a catastrophe they employ an army of Hous who rush forward if we so much as stumble on a stone, and who, if we are unlucky enough to cough, take our hands and lead us to hospital.

3 From the people's palace to the palace of the emperors

A thousand-mile journey starts with a single step. LAO TZU

Well before nine o'clock in the morning, Mr Hou is waiting for us in the hotel lobby, smiling, restless, eager to lead us as soon as possible to the attack on the New China.

He suggests Peking. First the Congress building, on the immense Tien An Men Square where the new régime's pride is on display. After that, because it is less important, we can see the Forbidden City, glamorous witness to imperial pride.

So it was that, as early as the day after our arrival, we were forced — in fact shocked — into awareness of the fundamental fact of the Chinese enigma: the power of numbers. This fact by itself is almost enough to explain all the grandeur and all the misery of the China of yesterday, of today, and probably of tomorrow. For great numbers, whether they are orderly or disorderly, always set in motion upheavals on their own scale.

In the morning we were going to visit the chamber of the Congress of the Chinese People's Republic: an amphitheatre where ten thousand people can sit in comfort and talk to each other in ten different languages. Decidedly there are a lot of people in this country! Whereas in the afternoon we would visit the seat of yesterday's governments: the Forbidden City with its multitude of rooms and its insoluble labyrinth of courtyards and corridors.

Like two heads facing each other through the arch of Tien An Men, these buildings symbolize the brain of the Chinese giant. From here in former days went forth the orders that caused the building of the Great Wall and the Grand Canal, and governed the most numerous and most ancient people on earth. From here today go forth the directives that harness the rivers and make the deserts green, and may make this people the most formidable industrial power in history. Here sits the multitude that gives orders to the multitudes.

But Mr Hou is in a hurry to get started. Let us follow him, then, to the Tung Chang An Chieh.

In building the famous Palace and Temple Quarter, the emperors indulged their taste for luxury and comfort; like the present rulers, they felt the need to build on a grand scale to overawe their subjects and to stagger foreigners. But at least it must be admitted that their architects had a certain sense of proportion.

One could not say as much for those who drew the plans for the Congress building. One might even suspect that they were not Chinese, since this gigantic coffee-cake recalls Soviet buildings. It is colossal and impressive, pretentious and phony. In a word, bourgeois.

But, unlike the Forbidden City of days gone by, of which the hungry people of Peking knew only the red walls, the Congress building is open to all. While we are there, several groups of Chinese and foreigners are visiting it.

First we cross an endless hall that leads to the Congress chamber. The guide, the interpreters, and Mr Hou reel off staggering statistics for us: all the information that is given to visitors to Rockefeller Center — except how many millions it cost.

Mr Hou wants us to admire the gilded friezes; but altogether the decoration of the building is not much better than the architecture. One beautiful thing, very simple: a great panel bearing a poem by Mao on the beauties of the Chinese landscape. In Chinese characters, black on white.

We visit a few of the many rooms bearing the names of provinces of China: the Szechwan room, with its bamboo marquetries, its exquisite watercolours, and its ancient vases; the Kwantung room, with its teak furniture, its jade statuettes, its porcelain flowers — such perfect imitations that one stoops to inhale their scent; the Liaoning room, with its lions carved in anthracite, its jade birds, and, above all, its immense watercolour — a propaganda painting in the current taste, yet beautiful.

Some artists of the régime succeed in painting blast-furnaces and muscular workers as delicately as they used to paint swallows perched on boughs of cherry-blossom.

After crossing a banqueting hall without pillars where five thousand guests can dine at once, we emerge to find a reassuringly fine blue sky.

We return to the hotel through quarters that are ancient but clean. We know Asia fairly well, yet we cannot remember finding a cleaner city there. One would look in vain for a cigarette-end or a bit of fruit-peel. Municipal employees, noses and mouths hidden by white gauze veils, sweep incessantly, even the streets that are not yet paved.

At lunch, two discoveries: a delicious dessert (quarters of apple cooked in caramel, which you dip in cold water before you eat them) and an English entomologist whom for no valid reason we christen McIntosh. He is a professor at Bristol University, and, like us, he has been invited here for a month or two. He is giving a few lectures and touring China.

With an entomologist, it was appropriate to discuss the question of flies, which strikes all foreign visitors. You have to know the Orient to appreciate the result of the régime's campaign against flies, the scourge of hot and populous countries. They say there are hardly any left in China; certainly, in three days we haven't seen a single one. McIntosh, who has been travelling across the country for a few weeks already, confirms that he has seen very few of them. The State, setting in motion its formidable instruments of propaganda, convinced 650 million Chinese that to kill a fly was a patriotic action; millions of fly-swatters immediately undertook the greatest massacre of flies since the Flood. It made you think.

In the afternoon, a pilgrimage to the source of the former grandeur of China: the Forbidden City, that is to say the complex of temples and imperial palaces cut off from Peking in the old days by a high wall capped with green or golden yellow tiles. Now it is a vast museum open to the people and to foreign visitors. The Chinese State has just spent millions to restore the Forbidden City.

Why this frenzy of restoration? The régime cannot deny history; it wants to prove that it respects art, and above all that it is the legitimate heir of the fabulous past of this country as old as the world. Just as, for example, the republicans of France made heavy sacrifices to restore Versailles, so the Communists of China are regilding the escutcheon of the Forbidden City, though it is the symbol of an abhorred régime.

We enter by the Tien An Men, majestic as a temple, closed by red doors studded with great gold nails. At first the roofs are all one sees, all one looks at: a sea of gleaming red roofs, blinding in the light. To rest the eyes and the spirit, one seeks refuge in one of the palaces, for example the Palace of Supreme Harmony where the emperor gave thanks to the gods for abundant harvests, the Palace of Future Happiness, the Palace of Perfect Peace.

The peace, the happiness, and the harmony are all bowled over by a band of tourists — friendly, noisy, laughing peanut-eaters and amateur photographers — in short, Americans visiting the Sainte-Chapelle. Only these Americans are Russians . . .

Well; let's escape to the Palace of Supreme Exaltation or the Palace of Exalted Harmony. Or, better, let's go and find the little Buddhist temple that seems deserted up there, on the mound called Coal Hill. There you find a disillusioned Buddha, weary of watching the Chinese file past him every Sunday, mocking him as if he were some imperialist fetish.

Let's thank Mr Hou.

'We have spent some unforgettable hours, thanks to you — *and* your emperors.'

But Mr Hou is deaf in that ear. 'The emperors did nothing in there. Those palaces were built by the people, by the misery of the poor and thanks to the ingenuity of the workers.'

Oh well, if he insists . . .

In the evening we are taken to a large department store. A quiet and amiable crowd flows through it without jostling. It's not an exhibition; everybody is buying. The only line-up is at the candy counter.

We look at the prices. We are startled by a fur hat marked at 750 yuan — $300. 'Who can buy that?' we ask the interpreter.

He has more sense of humour than Mr Hou. 'The Russian experts, I imagine! They're the ones with money.' But he pulls himself together at once. 'In the USSR they need hats like that. It's so much colder than here. Look. The ordinary hat the Chinese wear only costs 5 yuan [$2].'

To complete this already full day we go to the movies. Mr Hou had promised us a documentary on the conquest of the Himalayas by Chinese alpinists. He takes us to the wrong theatre and we undergo a Chinese torture: a Russian film dubbed in mandarin and translated into whispered English by an interpreter who certainly has more talent for Spanish.

4 A visit to Peking prison

If you rule the people by decree, and control them by the fear of punishment, they will do their best to avoid prison, but will have neither shame nor sense of honour.

— CONFUCIUS

We were promised a visit to the prison of Peking, and Mr Hou is as good as his word.

An assistant to the prison governor, a young Chinese who looks like a student at the Beaux-Arts, is waiting for us in the street, in front of the door. Just one sentry is on guard.

With a resigned smile our interpreter translates the greetings: very obsequious, very long, very Chinese. Within the walls, a garden welcomes us, planted with greenery and fine fragrant trees. This is a prison?

Here as everywhere else in China the tour begins with the obligatory cup of boiling-hot green tea and 'a few introductory words' from our host.

'This prison,' he tells us, 'was built forty years ago and reconstructed *after* the Liberation. We enlarged the cells and widened the windows to give the prisoners more air and light. We abolished bars.'

You only have to look: it's true, all right.

'Above all,' the assistant governor continues, 'we have changed the attitude to prisoners: instead of punishing them and humiliating them as *before*, we rehabilitate them by work and education.'

Education, in Marxist language, means Marxist education, among other things: to clear the head of old prejudices — the cause of all errors and crimes — and fill it with Marxism. On leaving, the prisoner will be transformed into a 'good citizen' by the standards of the New China.

The assistant governor makes no mystery of it. 'We try to convince the prisoners of the harm they have done society. We persuade them that all citizens must work, and that it is shameful to exploit the work of others by theft, fraud, etc. We give them lessons in politics, lectures on the domestic and international situations, explanations of the policy of the Great Leap Forward.'

'Is their leisure time organized?'

'Yes, of course. For instance, we take the prisoners out in buses — not wearing distinctive uniforms — to exhibitions and building projects so that they can see the achievements of the State. They take part in sports and amateur theatricals. They see films. They have books.'

'How do they fill their time?'

'One hour of recreation, two hours of study, eight hours of sleep, and eight or nine of work. There are rewards for good conduct: they are paid a small wage, and sometimes they are granted reductions in their sentences. Those who break prison regulations are reprimanded first. If that doesn't work they are put in solitary confinement. But there is never any physical torture.'

'Why not?'

'It was a practice of the old régime. Furthermore, we think the thing is to reform, not to punish. Physical torture is as ineffectual as it is inhumane. It doesn't make men better; that's done by work and education.'

Every question asked, every answer given, is carefully noted down by the assistant governor, by our guide, by our interpreter, and by another member of the prison staff, no doubt the political commissar. Our host will be thoroughly protected if we misquote him.

'How many prisoners have you?'

'Eighteen hundred, a hundred and ten of them women.'

'Political or criminal prisoners?'

'Both: Kuomintang agents, reactionary leaders, thieves, murderers —'

'Are the two groups kept separate?'

'No.'

'Are these long-term prisoners?'

'Mainly. The men sentenced to less than two years don't go to jail; they are rehabilitated by work, on farms.'

'Is there a staff psychiatrist?'

'No. A court doctor decides whether a convict should go to hospital or to jail.'

'Are some of the prisoners under sentence of death?'

'Yes, in two categories: those who are executed quickly because the people demand it and those who are to be executed two years after sentence. During those two years they have the chance of rehabilitating themselves and saving their lives.' (One imagines that some 'reactionary leaders' become excellent Marxists in less than two years . . .)

'How old are your youngest prisoners?'

'Eighteen. Younger offenders are sent to special schools; they are not considered criminals.'

'What are the commonest crimes in Peking?'

'Hmm . . . theft, corruption, murder. But that's decreasing.'

'Rape?'

'It's very rare.'

'Homosexuality?'

There is a long consultation. 'We have never heard of any.'

After this reassuring conversation, we do a leisurely tour of the vast and far from sinister prison. No bolts, no locks on the cell doors. Why escape, when it has become impossible to hide anywhere in this large country?

There are party slogans all over the walls. 'What does that one mean?' Hébert asks the interpreter.

'That the people want peace.'

Right next to it is a frightful chromo. We don't need the interpreter to translate the caption: a soldier is running his bayonet through the steel helmet of an American soldier.

We visit primitive but clean kitchens, where the soup smells very good. Then a number of workshops (cotton stockings, plastic things, radios) where the prisoners work in silence while a loudspeaker immerses them in revolutionary sayings and political speeches.

They are being re-educated . . .

At six o'clock, a banquet in a large restaurant that is renowned
for its lacquered duck, a Peking specialty. It is the Cultural
Association's official welcome to the Canadians, Australians, and
Americans. We, however, are in the majority, as there are only
two Australians — a Melbourne dentist and his wife — and two
Americans — a couple who have left the States, slamming the
door behind them, in protest against McCarthyism.

There are two round tables, in the Chinese manner. Trudeau
is seated in the place of honour with the president of the association, Mr Chu Tu-nan; Hébert and the others share the
table of the humbler sort with Mr Hou, all dressed up in navy
blue and freshly shaved.

The wine flows in torrents, especially as the Chinese have a
passion for toasts, which often degenerate into speeches, and
always end with a compulsory bottoms-up. After at least a dozen
of these, Mr Chu Tu-nan gives the signal for departure. We
must hurry, as we have seats at the Peking Opera.

WEDNESDAY, 21 SEPTEMBER

On the way to the urban commune of Ching Shan, Mr Hou is
beaming. At last he is going to show us an achievement that
puts the régime in the forefront of the Communist world.

This first visit to a commune — one of a special type —
interests us but leaves us puzzled. However, as we shall be touring other communes in the course of our journey, we shall keep
our comments until later.

Mr Hou presents us with a new interpreter, a fifth-year
student at the Institute of Foreign Languages. 'My name is Kao,'
he says with a broad smile. We had only had to mention to
Mr Hou that we would rather have a French-speaking interpreter; in less than twenty-four hours he found Kao, whose
guileless amiability and good humour were to make up for the
stiffness of our worthy 'commissar'. Nearly twenty years old,
graceful, and six feet tall, Kao speaks a well-articulated French,
plucked garden-fresh from *The Practical French-Chinese Conversation Guide*.

This evening he is to accompany us to a variety show given by the song-and-dance ensemble Yin Ue Ou Tao.

The open-air theatre, marvellously situated in the midst of the Forbidden City, is full to bursting. It is a fine open amphitheatre with a domed roof supported by elegant colonnades.

With almost comical professional conscientiousness Kao explains everything that happens on the stage; not very useful efforts since the show consists mostly of folk dances and folksongs. But he is suddenly solemn when he tells us the meaning of certain modern ballets, typical of today's productions in having only one purpose: to illustrate the General Line, to stimulate the Great Leap Forward, to serve official propaganda. Sometimes the movement is graceful, the propaganda less ponderous, and then it comes across. For instance, a number in which some young people launch a kite with propaganda messages for their brethren in Quemoy, the coastal island occupied by the Kuomintang. When the many-coloured kite has reached a certain height, a shadow replaces it in the blue sky of the setting. The shadow spins round and turns into an arrow, which then heads for a distant island and finally lands there: Quemoy.

But things soon degenerate into flat glorifications of the Red Army, production, and the frantic toil of a group of weavers prancing and mincing round a thermometer whose paper mercury predictably breaks through the top at the end.

The star turn is a mimed sketch. The scene is Taiwan. One of the characters, naturally, is a crudely caricatured G.I. Ostentatiously chewing gum, he tries to rape a Taiwan girl, symbolizing China. Peasants and workers come in, rescue the girl, and thrash the G.I. (who never stops moving his jaws). It brings the house down. Mao is vindicated.

All the same, it seemed to us that the 'patriotic' numbers were less enjoyed than the others. This restores our confidence in the good taste of the Chinese public.

5 The Chinese minorities

Men's natures are similar; it is their customs that divide them. — CONFUCIUS

THURSDAY, 22 SEPTEMBER

On the dot of 8.30, Mr Hou and Kao are pacing up and down in the hotel lobby. We did agree to meet them at 8.30; but we had made the mistake of counting on the legend that punctuality is not a characteristic quality of Orientals.

On the program is a semi-urban commune a few miles from Peking — Shu Ching Chan, which means the Commune of Sino-Soviet Friendship.

As expected, it all starts in a small reception room with tea, cigarettes, a director with statistics coming out of his pores, and secretaries who knock themselves out noting down the questions and answers. From the 'general explanations' of the director of the commune, we preserve a few figures that are astonishing but don't seem to us unlikely.

Within its fifty square miles this commune contains 178,000 inhabitants. Eighty per cent of the workers are in industry, twelve per cent in agriculture. Industrial activity centres on a metalworking factory. Our host tells us that its production has multiplied ten times since the organization of the commune in 1958. Now there are forty small satellite plants around the main factory, producing three hundred kinds of product, sixty per cent of them to supply the factory. They make electrical appliances, glassware, fertilizers, and agricultural machinery, as well as clothes and furniture for local consumption. Agricultural production supplies the people of the commune. Any surplus is put on the market.

There are in the commune ninety-five day-nurseries, 133 restaurants (although most of the workers eat at home), four homes for the fifty-one old people with no families, eleven medical clinics, thirty-nine free-service shops (such as shoe-repair, cleaning and pressing, and so on), twenty primary and six secondary schools, three movie theatres, fourteen television sets in public places, and fourteen amateur theatrical companies.

The director has finished his recitation, which he knows by heart from having had so many opportunities to perform it before foreigners since 1958. He asks if we have any questions to put before we tour the commune.

'Are there any women in your commune who prefer to stay at home and look after their children rather than have jobs in the workshops?'

'The women *want* to have jobs because of their awakened political consciousness. They loathe domestic work, and believe it their duty to help the new society; so they freely demand jobs. Before the Liberation, they often had to work in the fields, but they had to look after their children at the same time. Today their task is lighter, since they place their children in the community day-nurseries. Rare are those who refuse jobs; work is a glorious thing. And then they earn money and are less directly dependent on their husbands. This is *their* liberation!'

'Who decides the overall plan? Who tells you that this year you must produce more shoes and fewer hats? What proportions of your agricultural production are kept here, sold on the market, and contributed to the State?'

'First of all the State lays down the outline of the plan. Then all the people of the commune discuss it. Their elected representatives discuss it in their turn, and finally the State decides.'

'How many of these representatives are there?'

'The 178,000 members of the commune elect five hundred representatives, who form the assembly.'

'Is your commune intended to get bigger?'

'That's impossible; there are other communes all round ours.'

A broad smile from the director signals that the moment has come to begin the tour.

First, the workshops. In the first they are making — O mystery of planning — wax fruit! The methods are primitive, but the results aren't bad. Why tie up costly machinery when these merry old wives take real pleasure in playing at apple-tree and banana-tree?

In another workshop they are making charming nylon birds. In yet another, a hundred nimble little hands are transforming paper and cardboard into pretty Chinese lanterns.

Well, later on we saw things like this for sale in the large shops of Peking. How can you explain why a country that is short of everything can employ part of its labour force in the production of such frivolities? They tell us that the economy is now advanced enough to be able to satisfy even the whims of the Chinese consumer.

This explanation, certainly given in good faith, couldn't be the right one; it obliged us to meditate further on the mysteries of the Plan.

It is possible that the planners, having to find work for an innumerable labour force with few technical skills, encourage the production of non-utilitarian articles which can be sold in foreign markets in exchange for roubles, dollars, and other precious currencies. When these exports are going badly, they quite simply make up for it by flooding the local market with them and pushing their sale with large advertising posters. That's why we have been able to see, in the heart of a Communist country, billboards singing the praises of perfumed soap, just as in our capitalist cities; we would even bet that the radio and television have their soap operas.

But it's not all soap and skittles. Nearby, muscular men are making enormous metal gear-wheels. They make an impression in sand with a wooden die, pour molten metal from a local blast-furnace, let it cool, and finish the piece by hand, with crude files. To use such primitive methods in 1960, you must have a passion for industrialization, you must believe in the future . . .

The director marches us into a kindergarten. It's mealtime: chubby four-to-six-year-olds, manipulating chopsticks with consummate art, are stuffing themselves with a corn cake with bits of spinach baked into it, and taking great gulps of broth. We are tempted to take a taste: it's very good. But, confronted with so many running noses, we wonder if there isn't a period after their weaning when they lack vitamins.

Further on, a home for old people without families. They take our hands to show us their domain. As evidence of a bygone epoch, several old women have tiny atrophied feet, in the style of the old days. One of them serves us tea in the elegant drawing-room of what must have been the dwelling of a rich landowner before the Liberation; he won't have found mercy at the hands of the people's tribunal! There is a television set in the corner, some fine old pieces of furniture, and a few works of art — no doubt left behind by the former resident.

In these few hours we have seen very little of the Shu Ching Chan commune; enough, all the same, to be impressed by its drive, its organization, and above all its size. 'Isn't there some danger in such a big commune that the leaders will lose touch with the people?' Trudeau asks.

The director has an answer for everything. 'No. Every leader is obliged to work for one month in every year as an ordinary labourer, whether in a workshop or in the fields. It is an excellent way of keeping a sense of reality and staying close to the problems of the masses.'

Mr Hou never stops worrying about what we would like to see. Are we really satisfied with the program he is offering us?

'You mustn't be bored,' he says over and over again. 'Don't stand on ceremony,' says Kao ceremoniously.

As Canadians 'unlike the others', we are interested in the Chinese minority problem, and it is well known that Mao Tse-tung takes a lively interest in it.

'An excellent idea,' says Mr Hou. 'This afternoon, we will go to the Institute of Minorities of China.'

At some distance from the centre of Peking, we arrive in front of an imposing group of buildings, half hidden among young trees — 'planted *after* the Liberation by the students and professors themselves'.

At the door of the main building, which is in a vaguely Chinese style, we wait for the director of the literary division of the Institute.

Whoosh! — into the reception room: bulky armchairs, lace tablecloth, tea, cigarettes, 'explanations'.

'Our Institute was founded in 1951 — *after* the Liberation — to train the officials of the national minorities and to carry out the economic policy of the government in the minority regions. We have eight hundred instructors and twenty-six hundred students, drawn from forty-five minority groups.

'The Institute has four divisions. The political division teaches Marxism, political economy, the history of the Communist Party, and philosophy. The language division teaches about twenty of the minority languages. In the history division, history is taught — obviously — but also the social sciences. In the division of arts and literature, which I direct, we give courses in music, dancing, literature, painting, and so on. The courses are at university level and last four or five years.'

The tour that follows this obligatory lecture is interesting, because we go without warning into the lecture-rooms and even into the students' own rooms.

In the drawing studio we meet some Thais, who are earnestly drawing the head of Voltaire, whose plaster bust (after Houdon) is enthroned below the photograph of Mao.

The director abruptly opens a bedroom door, and we surprise a Tibetan girl of seventeen, with a very pretty face framed in two braids of black hair; she is playing the cello. In the next room we find an adorable Korean girl with enormous eyes who sings a folksong of her country at our request.

No question, this entire little world is eloquent of joie de vivre. Educated, housed, fed by the State, these young people have no cause for complaint against the régime; it is not surprising that, between a piano lesson and a folk dance, they apply themselves passionately to the study of Marxism.

The library is crowded: numbers of students are absorbed in reading huge books written in all sorts of non-Chinese languages. We speak to a Tibetan girl of less than twenty. 'What will you do later on, after you graduate?'

'What will be best for the country — what the party decides.' This is the total submission, the utter trustfulness of a novice in a religious community.

The periodicals room: students are reading the news of their own corners of the country in their own languages. There are even foreign newspapers, or more precisely Communist papers from foreign countries. We are proudly shown the *Daily Work-er*. Kao, who loves France, burrows feverishly in search of a French-language paper. At last he triumphantly brandishes *l'Humanité*. 'I read it every day at the Institute of Foreign Languages.' With complete ingenuousness, he adds: 'You too, I presume.'

Dear good Kao! His soul, so sensitive and so eager, is totally in the hands of the régime. Marxism, the Revolution, the Red Army, Mao: these are what fill his life. He has consecrated himself, just as among Christians a few elect souls consecrate themselves to God. No more room for doubt. He has found the truth. For the unhappy bourgeoisie of the whole world he feels a sort of benevolent pity. For Kao — and for others like him, whom in other times we might have 'bought' for ten cents in the name of the Holy Childhood — *we* are the pagans who need conversion.

All the same, he still respects us — and does us the honour of supposing that we read *l'Humanité* every morning.

'Foreign literature is here,' a librarian tells us proudly, pointing out a set of card-indexes. Trudeau goes up to it and puts his hand on one of the drawers. 'You are looking for something?' our guide asks helpfully.

'Yes,' the Leader answers, deadpan. 'I am looking for the works of Jacques Hébert. You are sure to have them all.'

The leg-pull is so outrageous that the most we expect is a mildly sarcastic word of apology. But Mr Hou and the librarian rush forward, with Kao hard on their heels.

'Certainly we have them. We'll look for them.'

Denis Lazure joins the game. 'No, first look for our Leader's book on the Asbestos strike.'

'Certainly!'

'It has been translated into Chinese?'

'There's no doubt of it at all,' says the librarian in perfect seriousness. And everybody burrows feverishly in the unlucky card-indexes.

Trudeau, the sorcerer's apprentice, has a great deal of trouble in putting a stop to these researches. He finally succeeds by dragging us towards the museum of the Institute, where we are struck by the infinite variety of habitats, costumes, jewels, and traditional implements in use among the minorities.

But already our thoughts are elsewhere. We are reflecting that, in comparison with China, all the peoples of the earth are minorities, and that there would be some profit in pondering on the underlying attitudes of the Chinese Communists when they confront the minority problem.

In the past, we had been tempted to dismiss as mere cold-war tactics the solicitude professed by the Chinese government towards colonial or exploited peoples throughout the world. But today's tour obliges us to reconsider the question; for we have witnessed the respectful caution with which the Chinese tackle the problem of their ethnic groups.

We are not naive enough to maintain that in such a matter the government of Chou En-lai is animated by the purest Christian charity. (Especially as Christian charity has always seemed to us singularly inoperative in the relations between Christian states and ethnic minorities; witness what we Canadians have done with our Indian and Eskimo population.) Undoubtedly Communist philosophy and strategy have ulterior motives in respecting minorities. But the fact remains that for all practical purposes minorities are better treated under such a philosophy than under Western régimes, where economic considerations take priority over all others.

Certainly we couldn't help smiling a little when, at that very moment, the director showed us a prayer-hall 'for our Moslem students', and a Buddhist chapel. Neither the one nor the other was exactly overcrowded; and we recognized the advantage for China in thus parading its tolerance before the Islamic and Buddhist nations of Africa and Asia. But it doesn't alter the fact that the minorities are over-represented at the governmental level in China itself: the fifty-one minorities, consisting of 38 million people, are only six per cent of the total population; yet they elect 14.5 per cent of the representatives in the Congress of the Republic.

It is clear, too, that, among all the students in the Institute of Minorities, the most important, the best prepared, and the most senior are those who are enrolled in the political division and who aspire to become high officials of the Party and of the State when they return to their minorities some day. (At present the minorities provide only four per cent of the members of the Chinese Communist Party.) All the same, the Institute eagerly welcomes those who only wish to become musicians, poets, or dancers. And, far from assimilating these minorities as much as possible (some of them consist of fewer than five hundred people), the powerful Chinese State does all it can to preserve their national characteristics, and notably their languages.

At the time of the Liberation, only twenty-one of the fifty-one minorities had written languages; the specialists in the Institute invented scripts for sixteen of them, and improved those of three others. Considering how complex the language problem is in China already, we cannot help respecting a policy that assumes the survival of new languages instead of taking the way of cultural assimilation.

Finally, chance led us to a conclusive indication. In studying the 'National Program for Agricultural Development', we read, in Article 24, that birth-control propaganda was to be carried on in all densely populated regions — *except those inhabited by national minorities.*

But we don't want to keep harping on the ethnic question, or Quebeckers may end up by thinking that Ottawa has more than one lesson to learn from Peking. One thing is certain: the present facts lead us to the conclusion that in the eyes of the Communist government the best way of integrating the minorities into the New China is not to try to assimilate them but — on the contrary, while respecting them — to seek to make them understand the blessings of Marxism.

6 The north-east, pride of New China

Everything has its beauty, though not everyone can see it.

— CONFUCIUS

Ten-thirty at night. We are leaving Peking for the industrial provinces (formerly Manchuria) which no visitor is spared, they are so proud of their blast-furnaces and factories.

The monumental new Peking Station is of an unheard-of luxury for China. Escalators and all. But the pretentious, fussy architecture would give Le Corbusier a stroke. Why would builders in a new country, determined to break with outworn traditions, not draw their inspiration from contemporary architecture? India and Brazil are no richer than China; but they build capitals beside which the new Peking is already outmoded — obsolete.

The immense station is almost empty. An off-hour? Useless to ask Mr Hou. He would tell us that the Chinese are too busy with the Great Leap Forward and have neither the time nor the inclination to travel.

We are led to our compartments in a first-class sleeping-car. 'There are no classes nowadays,' Mr Hou explains (we hadn't asked him a thing). 'There are different cars, that's all.'

The 'difference' is that virtually all travellers have to make do with wooden benches, while foreign visitors and a few important Chinese monopolize compartments with well-upholstered seats and comfortable berths. Our car is spotless — except for the toilets, where what one senses is not the blessings of the Revolution. Anything but.

FRIDAY, 23 SEPTEMBER

We walk through several of the 'different cars', where Chinese travellers are eating from their ricebowls, huddled on their wooden benches. In the dining-car there are only Europeans (Russian and Canadian tourists in this instance!) and a noble effort is made to serve 'European' cuisine.

The Russian tourists have finished their coffee. At a signal from their leader, the thirty-two comrades rise like automata and leave the car, bestowing shy smiles on the noisy, undisciplined bourgeois that we are. Trudeau sighs; not every leader has authority like that.

Changchun about 5 p.m.; a troupe of local dignitaries, mostly members of the Cultural Association, meets us at the station. Four cars are needed to take us all to the hotel. Another European meal. If our friends of the Association ever come to Canada, we'll stuff them with chop-suey!

SATURDAY, 24 SEPTEMBER

We were dreaming of a walk in Changchun, down long boulevards planted with trees and punctuated by traffic circles. But this is not Mr Hou's intention. From his point of view, the urgent thing is to visit the Railway Ministry's sleeping-car factory.

But we only just got out of a sleeping-car!

No fussing, please. Mr Cho Wen-kwe, chief engineer of the factory, is expecting us on the dot of nine; he has heaps of sleeping-cars to show us.

First of all they serve tea in thin glasses. Then they serve a one-hour lecture. We learn that, 'before', no sleeping-cars were manufactured in China. Since 1957 they have undertaken the construction of this imposing factory, according to Chinese plans and estimates. This is insisted on, for it mustn't be believed that the Chinese can do nothing without leaning on Soviet experts.

When the factory is finished it will produce 1600 sleeping-cars a year. For the moment they make do with a production of 150, which seems to keep five thousand workers busy. Later on there will be ten thousand.

Next, the tour. There are miles of factory. It's mad to tour all that on foot when there are so many sleeping-cars, completely empty.

Actually, the plant itself seems half empty. Under the high domed roofs of these gigantic buildings, we are plunging at one moment into swarms of machines and workers, buzzing with activity; the next, we are picking our way round stacks of scrap-iron and accumulations of half-finished parts; the next, we are crossing vast spaces, which would be absolutely empty were there not above our heads a powerful travelling crane, manoeuvred by a Juliet who surveys us from her balcony with great almond eyes.

Heavy industry in China makes us think of a child dressed up in his father's clothes. He seems lost inside them, a bit ludicrous; but he knows the future will take care of all that.

Even more than the other day, when we watched a commune making its agricultural implements right from the smelting of the pig-iron, we are convinced that we are witnessing the beginning of an industrial revolution. Today's scene is less moving, less touching, but more conclusive. We have no doubt that in a little while — never mind whether it is one year or five — this factory will be filled to bursting with people and machines working in real co-ordination with the single purpose of exceeding their quotas.

Already most of the machines are Chinese; those with Soviet and Swedish marks are in the minority. As for manpower, there is an inexhaustible human reservoir to draw on once it can be taught the necessary skills. Notice the frail-looking technician with the long braids over here: she is squatting beside two strapping youths who are watching attentively as she shows them with a piece of chalk how to solve their problem.

But in the meantime the tour is going off the rails: the chief engineer is taking us by a route designed to prevent all anxiety about time-and-motion or suspicion of a production line. Parts are piling up in confusion beside the machine that has produced them; when the heap gets too big, the machine is stopped and the workers are sent away — to the fields? to have a rest? to other machines? — who knows?

Nothing in our unusual stroll prepares us for its miraculous conclusion: at the eleventh hour, a group of workers put the innumerable parts together — and a sleeping-car suddenly materializes before our very eyes! It may not be creation in the full philosophical sense, but it is very close to it.

Our emotions oscillate between incredulity and enthusiasm. It is the latter that finally carries the day; so much so that we have a good mind to offer to pay for the next round — of green tea. Anyway, the atmosphere encourages enthusiasm: as in all factories in the New China, there are so many slogans on the walls, pennants, flags, and paper ribbons that you would think it was a holiday. It's all part of a very effective system for stimulating the workers to emulation. Everywhere are posters filled with numbers and adorned with multicoloured designs. Among the doves and five-pointed stars are flowers, and fire-breathing dragons: the Old China is rearing its head.

The tour ends as it began, with the ritual glass of tea. 'Have you any advice to give us?' asks the chief engineer, so seriously that we manage not to smile.

'No, really — '

'Please don't hesitate. Any criticism you have would help us. We lack experience, and we know that Canada is very advanced in the sleeping-car field. I should be most happy to hear your suggestions.'

That'll teach us to go to China without having visited Canadian Car and Foundry! The only way out of the impasse is to ask questions. 'How many foremen have you in the factory?'

'None. It is the Communist Party cell that directs the work. There is no real supervision; heads of departments direct, but don't supervise.'

'What do you do about unsatisfactory workers?'

'If a worker is deficient in skill, we give him evening courses. If it is his spirit that is bad, we educate him. It would be quite useless to dismiss him, because anywhere else in China he would find the same employer — the State. His own section will discuss his case before submitting it to management, which will decide what measures to take. It is the section that will judge whether one worker has improved, whether another deserves higher wages; but management makes the decisions.'

'May a worker ask for higher wages himself?'

'The wage is set by the Plan according to ability, but it is the section that rates the abilities of its members. Notice that men and women get the same wages. In addition, good workers are rewarded by bonuses equal to ten or even twenty per cent of their wages.'

'If a machinist demands higher wages than, say, the painters and doesn't get them, can he leave?'

'He can, but it won't do him any good; in fact, the wage-scales (real wages, I mean) are the same in all parts of China, taking account of variations in the cost of living from one region to another.'

'What would happen if a group of machinists, dissatisfied with their treatment, decided to leave or go on strike?'

'I have never heard of a case. The scale of wages was studied for a long time. In 1956, the workers of every region discussed the wage question for six months; then the State set the rates, taking account of working conditions. Miners, for instance, are better paid than carpenters because their working conditions are harder.'

'Are promotions based on seniority or ability?'

'Ability.'

Two-thirty. A visit to the big film studio, one of the four important studios of China. Tea, and a very talkative director. 'After the Liberation,' he begins — with no prompting —, 'the Soviets turned this studio over to us. (It was built under the Japanese occupation.) We produce feature films and documentaries that are exported to fifty countries. Besides that, we have dubbed about four hundred foreign films, from twenty-two countries.'

'What is your general policy?'

'To follow the directive of Chairman Mao, that is to say to put art into the service of the soldiers, workers, and peasants. Our prime task is to describe the Great Leap Forward. We have also made many historical films and newsreels. A favourite theme is the struggle against imperialism. The people are encouraged to write scenarios; some soldiers and workers have written excellent ones. All in all, we obey the watchwords of the Communist Party, but it is the masses who are responsible for our success. Just now there is a lot of enthusiasm among the actors who are preparing a series of films to commemorate the fortieth anniversary of the foundation of the Chinese Communist Party. But we lack experience, there are still weaknesses, and if you would be kind enough to give a little advice . . .'

We go through a studio where work is in full swing; but nobody seems to be disturbed, not even the lovely Being-Yang — a great Chinese artiste, we are told. Between takes she favours us with broad smiles, then at once resumes a tragic air and utters some historic sentence. She wears the Red Army uniform and is leading a band of dust-covered extras to certain victory against Chiang Kai-shek's bandits. In everyday life she is a member of Congress.

It seemed appropriate to ask the director a few questions on the 'Hundred Flowers' policy which had briefly been expected to relieve the intellectual and artistic constipation of the New China. 'Let a hundred flowers bloom,' Mao had said in May 1956, 'and let a hundred schools of thought contend.'

'That means — what, exactly?'

'A hundred flowers — that is to say that all styles, all methods of expression can be used. A hundred schools — that is to say . . . that the party line must be followed. Artists may produce whatever they like, except anti-socialist works or works aimed against the party line. A hundred schools — that means that hundreds of groups may express themselves in their own way and compete to produce even better films for the people. And within each group there are several styles of expression. A hundred schools . . . all schools are good, except the bourgeois ones.'

Now, is that clear, or isn't it?

'What if weeds grow up among the flowers?'

'They must be allowed to grow, and then be torn up for compost. Our success in the arts stems from this policy.'

All very clear. As Lu Ting-yi, propaganda director of the Communist Party, said in 1956: 'Literature and art *must praise* the new society and positive people. But at the same time it *must criticize* the old and negative elements. . . . In the choice of subjects, *prohibitions* and *directives* can only frustrate art and literature, and produce platitudes in bad taste.'

'And do you pay well for scenarios?'

'A good scenario earns its author 5000 yuan [$2000], a mediocre one 3000 yuan [$1200], and others [bad ones?] about 1000 yuan [$400].'

'Who decides how many films you will make in a year, and what the budget will be?'

'The Ministry of Cultural Affairs. This year it decided that we would make eighty-four films in China, twenty-four of them in our studio. We are trying to exceed that objective.'

Next they offer to show us a film produced in Changchun. We have heard of one film, which has had its hour of fame — *Shee-er (The Girl with White Hair)* — and we ask if it is possible to see it.

'It's already a little out of date. We have made better ones since. But if that is your wish — '

So we are shown *The Girl with White Hair*.

7 One factory after another

He who does not reflect, and does not lay his plans far in advance, will find difficulties at his door. — CONFUCIUS

SUNDAY, 25 SEPTEMBER

A visit to a carpet factory. Reception room, tea, cigarettes, large photograph of Mao, explanations by the director.

Oh, it's interesting, of course. Carpets. Thousands of yards of carpet produced since the Liberation. Improvement in the quality of carpets. The carpet looms, the women who brush and the women who cut the carpets. Carpets that are rolled up, carpets that are exported to the four corners of the earth; carpets, all those carpets . . . *(But it's such a fine day outside!)* 'Since Chairman Mao's Great Leap Forward, production has doubled, tripled, quadrupled, quintupled — '

The director is in top form. The whole world is going to be covered with carpet! Wall to wall . . .

'Results like this can be explained only by the extraordinary enthusiasm of the workers. Many of them experienced the capitalist exploitation of the old days. Now they think of themselves as belonging to one big family, and as working for it. They know that those of them who want to learn more can take evening courses. They are happy.'

Well, how can you verify this kind of cheerful statement, such as we have heard every day since we got here? All the same, it is clear that the small-wage earner is no longer a mere pariah, as he was before. They are trying in every possible way to interest him in public affairs, in the new ideology, in the industrial revolution. They have succeeded at least in convincing him that he is no longer just a speck of dust in the proletarian mass, and that he is part of this revolution; that without him China wouldn't be the power it has become in the last eleven years. How could the Chinese worker fail to feel a certain pride? How could he fail to be disconcerted if he could read the un-

ceasing lamentations of Western journalists over the fate of the
nameless forced labourers of the New China?

That there are slave-labour camps is a hypothesis that for
obvious reasons we can neither confirm nor deny. What is
certain is that the mass of Chinese workers are living better
than they ever have before. It is for these workers above all
that new housing developments have been built, with clean
dwellings, recreational centres, rest-houses in the country. All
this they owe to the régime; they know it, and they are given
no chance to forget it.

It's Sunday. As we come out of the carpet factory, we suddenly ask Mr Hou to take us to the Catholic church of Changchun.

The church is empty. There is holy water in the basins and
the lamp is alight in the sanctuary. Let's go and knock on the
presbytery door. 'We're sorry. The priests are in the country.
They are helping with the harvest.'

In the afternoon, history takes on reality for us when we are
taken to see an immense automobile factory, whose construction
began — with help from the USSR — in 1953, and whose assembly line produces tractors, trucks, cars, and station wagons.

The Chinese are so proud of the four-ton truck of Changchun
that its picture is on banknotes. According to the plan, the
factory must make fifty of these vehicles in eight hours, with
23 thousand employees and ten thousand machine tools. Since
the impetus given by the Great Leap Forward, production has
tripled, and has been diversified.

A lengthy tour of the factory. Through the infernal racket of
power hammers, drills, and riveting machines, there bursts from
time to time the gentler racket of a small improvised band, mainly of percussion instruments; it is a team of workers marching,
with a flag at their head, to challenge another team to a production duel.

Mr Hou is red with pleasure, and Kao is very pink at least,
when we are shown the factory's latest masterpiece: a beautiful
deluxe automobile, the Cadillac of the New China — though it
reminds us more of a Ford. The name of this marvel — which

they took a long time to choose — is the Red Flag. Its finish
strikes us as elegant: enough chrome to fool an American consumer, and ornaments in ivory instead of plastic.

Red Flags are being made only when urgently needed by high
officials who are tired of going for outings in Chevrolets 'made
in USA'. For the moment the important thing is to supply this
country, in the full swing of its industrial revolution, with the
thousands of trucks it needs so badly. We watched these trucks
coming off the end of the assembly line in a steady rhythm —
inelegant but sturdy. A driver would climb into the cab, turn
the key, and — after testing the horn rather insistently — drive
the vehicle into a parking lot from which it would soon head
for Mongolia or Sinkiang. We kept count, watches in hand: the
director was not exaggerating when he told us that the factory
produced fifteen to twenty an hour.

We keep thinking of the automobile industry of Canada,
which in 1956 refused orders from China even though its workers in Windsor were unemployed. We keep thinking of this
market, lost — in deference to the feelings of the State Department — to the profit of the Polish, Czech, Russian, and German
factories, whose cars you see everywhere in China. In fact, you
even see a certain number of late-model American cars; could
it be that some American companies are doing indirectly what
they forbid their Canadian subsidiaries to do?

The visit concludes in the obligatory way, in a vast reception
room where we have tea under the paternal eye of a plaster
Mao, perched on a sort of altar covered in red felt. The director
asks if we have questions, criticisms, or (why not?) advice to
give the engineers.

Advice? No. But maybe this is the moment to ask for an
explanation of certain oddities of technological organization. The
engineer is young, he spent several years in the USSR, and he
even replies pleasantly enough to the few Russian sentences we
throw at him. So let's go on with our problems. 'On the out-
skirts of the plant we noticed tractor engines left out in the
rain. Isn't that a sign of something of a production bottleneck?'

'Not at all. That's because our architects didn't build enough
shelters to take care of our tremendous production.'

'But that in itself is surely a kind of bottleneck, due to bad planning. Besides, we have seen dozens of other examples: for instance, a corridor of the factory was so cluttered with generators piled up all anyhow that a backing truck couldn't help damaging several of them.'

'Which only goes to show that the teams concerned with the production of generators [and of tractor engines] have exceeded the quota. They're good workers.'

'Good workers whom you're going to have to lay off while the other teams catch up with this overproduction.'

'They certainly won't be laid off. They will go and help the teams that aren't as far ahead in making the other components of the tractor or truck. And equilibrium will be restored.'

'From the technological point of view, isn't this bumpy way of reaching equilibrium almost as inefficient and costly as lay-offs? You will surely admit that a well-co-ordinated plan must aim at producing, in a given time, four wheels, one body, one engine, one generator, two headlights, one horn, and so on, so that the assembly line will produce one truck in the given time without overproduction of some parts or a shortage of others.'

'That's not the way we do it in China; the workers are so enthusiastic that they keep on exceeding their quotas.'

The political commissars (for, aside from Mr Hou, there were always a few of them at these interviews) are delighted; the 'capitalists' thought they had found an error in planning, but they have been stopped short before the clear superiority of the Chinese worker. Our engineer is no doubt happy to find that his replies have satisfied the comrades; he may even hope that he has dazzled the Canadian visitors; but he is too intelligent to believe in his explanations himself.

Once again we are forced to the conclusion that the officials who talk to us are generally disingenuous. The loss is theirs: it will compel us to take with reservations any information whose accuracy we cannot verify from our own observation.

Yet we can't bring ourselves to believe it is simply a matter of lying. In the discussion just quoted, what motive could the engineer have had to hide the truth from us? It would have been so simple to say: 'When industrialization is in its infancy and the labour force is still green, it is impossible to foresee the exact production of a given team assigned to a given machine (generators, for instance). Everybody is an apprentice and everybody competes with his neighbour; those who are behind exert themselves to catch up with the front-runners. Until standards of performance are empirically established, the technical directors are reduced to planning by guesstimate. Each successive step in the plan will correct the mistakes of the last; and when the optimum production figures are known we will be in a position to assign to each part of the truck the exact number of men to prevent overproduction and bottlenecks.'

But the engineer chose to tell us stories instead. Why? We are tempted to think that he wanted to 'save face' — that blanket explanation for use whenever the Orient passeth all understanding. Manifestly, the Chinese Communists have a horror of admitting to a foreigner that they can possibly make a mistake or that there can be any flaw in their system.

In any case, once more we are free to record that our Chinese hosts are not to be taken seriously when, after a tour or a journey, they tell us 'We have our weaknesses . . .' and ask for our criticisms.

The factory is completely surrounded by a red-brick housing estate. We ask to visit a worker's apartment, and we are allowed to choose. So we pick at random, and go into a three-room apartment occupied by a couple in their forties with four children. It has a kitchenette and two rooms, each serving as bedroom and living-room combined. The husband has a job in an engine-manufacturing workshop, and his wife is an inspector of finished products.

While they are telling us about their work with enthusiasm — real or assumed for the benefit of the capitalist visitors — we study the tiny apartment. Few families of six in Canada would put up with it, even though there are plenty of workers in our rich country living in squalid slums. 'Modest' isn't the word for the furniture. (No thirty-six months to pay here.) There is hot water, gas for cooking, central heating. No television (it will come soon), but an impressive radio, an alarm-clock, a huge thermos so that hot tea will always be available,

foliage plants, a few family photographs (including Daddy Mao).
The employees of General Motors (when they are actually working) live better than their brethren of the Changchun automotive
works. But in what other Asian country do the workers live as
well as the latter?

In the evening, a banquet given by the provincial Cultural Association. For once the representative of the Association, a hard
drinker, has a sense of humour.

Often they take advantage of these banquets to serve up,
between the sea-slugs and the preserved eggs, a rigmarole of
party slogans that by now we all know by heart. Thanks to the
heady red wine of the district, good humour quickly gets the
better of the Great Leap Forward and the Hundred Flowers. By
the soup course (which is towards the end of the meal) we relax
to the point of singing Canadian *chansons*, which Kao translates
as best he can. He is quite embarrassed by Trudeau's repertoire,
and is deeply puzzled to learn that to afford a drink in our
capitalist country one must

vendre le jupon de sa blonde . . .

By the dessert course, the Great Leap Forward is several laps
behind. But when our Chinese friends at last start singing, Kao
has to confess that the chorus celebrates the Great Leap Forward!

In the next room a party of Brazilian doctors is being entertained. When a few French words float towards their table, they
sympathetically intone the 'Marseillaise'. We join in the chorus,
to the great astonishment of the Chinese. A tenth toast, to the
henceforth indestructible friendship of China, Brazil, and
Canada, settles everything.

Our hosts accompany us to the Changchun station, where we
are to take the night train for Shenyang, which the Japanese
called Mukden.

MONDAY, 26 SEPTEMBER

Half asleep, still heavy with wine and talk, we arrive in Shenyang at 3.30 in the morning. It is hardly credible, but the representatives of the local Cultural Association are there, shivering

on the platform. At the hotel, before we go to bed, we have to drink tea with these charming people, and express in language as flowery as possible the joy we feel at arriving in the beautiful city of Shenyang that . . . which . . . whose . . .

Are there any people in the world more hospitable than the Chinese?

And at *nine o'clock* in the morning Mr Hou will be waiting for us in the lobby, determined to make us tour, according to the program, 'Factory Number One for the manufacture of machine tools'. This factory, built by the Japanese in 1935 for the assembly and repair of tanks, is said to have been dismantled in 1946 by the Kuomintang, who sold the machinery and turned the workshops into stables. At the Liberation only twenty old German machines remained. With the help of Soviet experts, the factory was rebuilt and refitted. Seventy per cent of the present machines come from the USSR, the rest from other Communist countries. The chief product is lathes, of all sizes.

As a rest from factories, we long to dream awhile before the tomb of an emperor, or the tranquil Buddha of some pagoda lost in the mountains. But that's the past, and Mr Hou, like all the Mr Hous in China, thinks only of the present, dreams only of the future. When we ask our hosts to identify some modern building, they reply enthusiastically: 'It's a hospital, it's a library — built *after* the Liberation.'

'And that lovely temple, on that little hill over there?'

'I don't know — some temple . . .'

'Buddhist?'

'Perhaps.'

It doesn't interest them.

8 How to make doctors & steel

To impose one's will on others, that is force. — LAO TZU

MONDAY, 26 SEPTEMBER

In the afternoon we are offered a hospital, which is also a medical school. The building dates from 1929. The assistant dean, or deputy director, welcomes us in a large Victorian reception room: dark panelling, fat leather armchairs, green plants that show no inclination to bloom. Mao is doubly present, in a photograph in a heavy frame and in a white plaster bust. But it is especially in the remarks of the assistant dean that his presence makes itself felt. We would like him to talk medicine, but he insists on talking politics. He rattles off statistics: 'Four hundred professors, four thousand students, a library of 240,000 volumes, forty-three departments for the study of medicine. But we also teach Marxism-Leninism and the works of Chairman Mao. One day a week is given to the subject.'

'Is this useful in the care of the sick?'

'It is useful for raising the level of consciousness of doctors-to-be. In every matter we apply the policy of the Communist Party as expressed by Chairman Mao. For instance, he has said: "Study must be combined with manual labour and must serve the working class." That is why our students do eight weeks a year of manual labour, in the factories or the fields. We want them to take full account of this reality: work created the world, the workers are masters of the world.'

Between two flights of this nature, the assistant dean notices that Micheline Legendre is wearing a bandage on her foot: she sprained her ankle the day before yesterday as she was coming out of an arena where we had seen an excellent basketball game. Sensation! There is an anxious consultation. 'We absolutely must take an x-ray,' says the assistant dean.

The x-ray reveals that a small piece of bone in the ankle has been chipped off: a tiny fracture. General consternation. Surgeons are sent for, and they discuss it steadily for a good quarter-hour. At last they suggest either making a plaster cast in the Western manner, or treating the fracture by the traditional Chinese method, that is by applying a poultice of herbs instead. The assistant dean assures us that the Chinese method would be more effective and less of a hindrance to the patient — who wouldn't after all want to drag a plaster cast across China. Even with a poultice she should avoid walking for two or three days.

Micheline Legendre opts unhesitatingly for the Chinese solution. (She was never to regret it, especially as they gave her opium as a sedative.)

We put on white smocks for the tour of the hospital — which is very well organized, Dr Denis Lazure assures the rest of us. There is even a small laboratory where researches in Pavlovian theory are carried on with the collaboration of an unlucky dog, which looks as if it isn't having much fun. The first dog we have seen in China, by the way.

In the library we find recent numbers of all the leading medical journals — American, English, French, German, Soviet.

Our curiosity is especially aroused in the part of the hospital devoted to acupuncture. For, though they teach modern medicine in all the Chinese medical schools, they don't neglect the teaching of traditional Chinese medicine. 'We follow the watchword of Chairman Mao,' explains the assistant dean. 'He has said: "We must learn Chinese medicine and preserve our precious heritage." ' A five-thousand-year-old heritage.

We are invited to watch a treatment. The patient is a woman who has been deaf for several months. The specialists have given the case up; the diagnosis is psychological deafness. Acupuncture is called for: such an apparently simple method that it is hard to think it scientific. The treatment consists of sticking fine needles into the skin. Anatomical charts indicate the ninety-six spots on the body, which when tickled by the right needles will give new vitality to one organ or another. In the present case it is in the lobe of the ear that they have planted a very short needle, attached to a ring.

Here is another patient, who has at least ten needles in one knee: a case of rheumatism. For some diseases they also use a medicinal herb called *ai* which is applied to the skin and burned.

Old wives' remedies? The fact remains that scientists of every country, without explaining them, concede the astonishing results obtained by acupuncture. In fact they were first made famous by Pavlov.

Back to the English drawing-room and the paramedical reflections of the assistant dean. 'The student who has bourgeois ideas is re-educated on the job in the socialist spirit. Everybody helps him. He is made to do manual work until it has transformed him ideologically.'

'Can a doctor choose the town where he will practise?'

'No. The State will decide for him, according to need.'

'Is private practice allowed?'

'No. All doctors work in hospitals, in the service of the State.'

To our utter astonishment, Mr Hou, who has never before opened his mouth when we are talking to an official, suddenly declares: 'Doctors who come from the working class or the peasant class are better. They serve the people better than doctors with bourgeois intellectual backgrounds.' He watches us to make sure we are taking notes.

Taken aback for a moment, the assistant dean continues. 'We have to refuse a large number of candidates every year. Last year we accepted only six hundred out of two thousand, for lack of places.'

'What standards do you apply in accepting candidates?'

'The very first step is a political examination. Next we take account of the students' general knowledge and the state of their health.'

This evening, another banquet. Our host is a charming old gentleman, vice-president of the Cultural Association of Shenyang and director of the Agricultural Institute. He speaks English. For the first time since our arrival, we chat with a Chinese without an interpreter. (Dear Kao is not put out at all; in fact he's delighted.) We learn that he studied agriculture in

Minnesota for seven years. He even knows Canada — he has
visited Winnipeg.

As usual, toast follows toast at an alarming tempo — all the
more alarming since this is our initiation in sorghum alcohol, a
formidable variety of rotgut with a most suspicious taste. To
revive us, no doubt, they hand each of us one of the scalding-
hot damp towels with which the Chinese love to wash their
faces at the end of a meal.

About 9 p.m., off for Anshan by train. We leave Micheline
Legendre in Shenyang with our English-language interpreter, the
gentle Yong — with the face that is half smile and half
spectacles.

At Anshan the representatives of the Association are on hand
— speeches, official cars, and all. The hotel is clean and dull, but
in our rooms we are sure to find hot tea, and Chinese slippers
and kimonos. Let's sleep; we have been promised *four* factories
tomorrow!

TUESDAY, 27 SEPTEMBER

Followed by a rather subdued Kao, Mr Hou bursts into each of
our rooms. 'Quick! It's late. You are waited for downstairs.' For
him this is perhaps the most important day of the whole trip;
on the program is a tour of the great steelworks of Anshan,
pride of the New China. Carpet factories and sleeping-car
factories are all very well; but the steelworks of Anshan are the
very key to the economic future of the country.

To save time one of the managers of the factory has come
right to the hotel to give us the 'few explanations'. He is already
waiting for us in one of the lounges — hence Mr Hou's flap.

'All the surrounding mountains are full of rich ore,' the little
man tells us enthusiastically. 'It has been mined for two
thousand years. The Japanese organized its exploitation in the
imperialist way, that is they just mined the ore and made half-
finished products for export to Japan. It was a systematic policy:
raw materials in China, industry in Japan.' (For Quebeckers this
has a faintly familiar ring . . .) 'In 1949 the government gave
the word: top priority to heavy industry. The whole country

rallied to the support of Anshan. Factories razed by the Japanese were rebuilt, the workers were summoned back from the surrounding countryside. And in 1957 the annual production reached 2,900,000 tons of steel. The workers toiled with amazing enthusiasm. And it was noticeable that improvements in technique went hand-in-hand with emancipation of thought. For instance, the compressor plant, which according to the overall plan was supposed to produce 300,000 tons, produced 900,000. Another example: the engineers said it would take twelve months to build a blast-furnace and put it in working order. The planners asked the workers to build one in less than ten months. Well — such a fine spirit prevailed that it was built in four.'

There follows a series of equally impressive examples. 'In short, this year we have already produced 5,500,000 tons of steel, including 4,200,000 tons of construction steel. And the Anshan factory, integrated into a complete ironworking complex of forty-nine plants, plays a prime role in the spread of socialist enlightenment in China. Another of its tasks is to support, by supplying personnel and by making plans and estimating costs, the construction of new ironworking centres. In this way it has provided other centres with seventy thousand people by now.'

We ask about wages.

'*Before* the Liberation, they used to earn seventeen yuan [$6.80] a month. Now they earn more than forty-one [$16.40]. The standard of living is constantly rising. In the last few years we have put up housing for a hundred thousand people, quite apart from the usual services: a free medical service, restaurants, night schools, day-nurseries, kindergartens — and a special diet (meat and eggs) for workers assigned to especially arduous labour.'

Fortified by these 'few explanations' — which we have greatly condensed here — , off we go to the inferno of the steelworks. If one still had any doubts about the rapid rise of China to the rank of a very great power, they would vanish here.

Admittedly the appearance of the industrial equipment is discouraging. For instance, the blast-furnace that was built in four months is in full production, but it already has a terribly dilapidated look; the brickwork is crumbling in places, an iron ramp is twisted. And there are heaps of scrap-iron lying about in the most unlikely places. Even when we see something brand new we notice broken tiles or unsightly patched-up repairs. In short, the factories seem to be no more built for permanence than the dormitory buildings.

It would be useless to question the Chinese about the reasons for such a state of things; they would be deeply wounded. But a little reflection gives us a likely explanation. At the very beginning of the industrial revolution, the initial impetus must be given by means of such technicians and skilled labour as are available — that is, almost none. In consequence, the construction workers are organized in mobile teams to serve vast regions. They move in quickly, build quickly, and quickly move on to the next place; they haven't the time to come back and fuss about maintenance. The concept that lies behind this pace is imposed by necessity: if you waited till you could do perfect work, you'd never get started.

This need to get started quickly accounts for a number of other aspects. Certain heavy tasks are performed by women, or by adolescents of whom one can hardly believe that they have reached the legal minimum age of eighteen. The question to ask oneself is always whether their present condition is more acceptable than it was before, and, further, if the plan calls for improvement in the future. For in social as in economic affairs it is the *tempo* of growth that counts in the long run. What really matters is not that there are still Soviet technicians, machines made in Poland, and whole factories that were originally built and equipped by the Japanese. The striking thing is that the Chinese are getting the best possible value out of all this while they adjust themselves to big industry with admirable adaptability. In the midst of this inferno we have seen tiny slips of girls, twenty years old and with angelic expressions, manipulating powerful cranes as if they were sewing machines, dextrously controlling great magnets that lift and stack tons of glowing rails.

'Why isn't this kind of work entrusted to a man?'

'Because that one is the best-qualified worker.'

When you approach a worker his face lights up; he is proud of being so important, of understanding the difficult skills of ironworking, the formidable secrets of steel, just as well as the specialized workers of Sheffield, Pittsburgh, or Magnitogorsk. This proud man bears little resemblance to the slave portrayed by the anti-Chinese propaganda that prevails in the West. Moreover, how could the tremendous progress, of which the Anshan steelworkers are only one example, have been achieved in eleven years by slave labour? The genius of Mao is to have persuaded hundreds of millions of people — by astoundingly effective methods — of the grandeur and nobility of their task.

In fact, we are inclined to say that this is the most remarkable success of the Chinese Communist Party: that it has conveyed to — or imposed on — the Chinese people confidence in the future and an active faith in their own destiny. The government has given the Chinese a job to do, and *gets them to do it* — which is a considerable innovation when you think of the fatalistic and unworldly China of the past.

One may disagree with the methods used; one may reject the governing principles; one may be repelled at the thought of such a system ever being established in Canada; but in a world dominated by power politics such attitudes are apt to be swept aside as the nice scruples of comfortable people. If China, with its afforestation projects, can make the Gobi Desert fertile; if China can overcome droughts and floods by its indefatigable construction of canals and dams; if China succeeds in building its industrial progress on its inexhaustible reserves of manpower and natural resources — and even one short visit served to show us what energies were being mobilized for these tasks — then China's methods are going to be imitated by the two-thirds of the human race that goes to bed hungry every night. And the moral indignation of the West will be powerless to stop it.

The government never ceases to contrive new activities to keep hands and minds occupied. Long before one slogan has lost its force another is invented to whip up popular enthusiasm. In this way the Communist Party always has ready some new triumph to astound the people.

China is a country on the march. Of course the Party makes

mistakes; we have pointed some of them out in these pages. Of course natural calamities are going to throw out their calculations; we have seen proof of that recently. Of course the people are eventually going to get out of breath from running this relentless race; you only have to think of the refugees arriving every day in Macao and Hong Kong. But any anti-Communist who founded his hopes on this would be crazy. Six hundred and fifty million Chinese are a good part of the world. And the Communist Party isn't out of breath, and it isn't running away. Not it.

9 All the Chinese work

Politics is war without bloodshed while war is politics with bloodshed. — MAO TSE-TUNG

Back to Peking. This time we stay in a different part of town, at the Chen Mein Hotel. Because we had told Mr Hou that the minorities problem interested us, he had given us a tour of the Institute of Minorities. Fearing that that would not suffice to convince us of the excellence of the New China's policy in this matter, he takes us to the Palace of Minorities, comprising numerous enormous exhibition halls, each dealing with a subject affecting one or other of the fifty-one Chinese minorities.

Most of our time is spent on the Tibetan floor, where an army of Lolitas, equipped with pointers, serve their country by reciting official truths in front of posters, maps, and photographs.

It is a rather naive exhibition; a cream separator and a small tractor are on display, simply to establish the fact that similar articles have been sent to the backward people of Tibet, so lately wrested from the domination of a 'corrupt, feudal, and bourgeois' ruling class. All the guides take every opportunity to denounce the 'nationalist bourgeois chauvinism' of these ruling classes. Since Trudeau has shown some anxiety to know the meaning of this curious concoction, the guides have a long consultation, and then announce: 'The director of the Palace will explain that very soon, just before you leave.'

Clearly these nice girls are reciting their lessons on the minorities in the same way our Quebec schoolchildren chant the definition of transsubstantiation. But Mr Hou is on the qui vive, and we have the opportunity to observe that he knows his Mao Tse-tung. His explanations repeat almost word for word a speech Mao made in February 1957 ('On the Correct Handling of Contradictions Among the People'): 'It is absolutely necessary to establish good relations between the Hans [i.e., the Chinese majority] and the national minorities. . . . In certain regions, Great-Han chauvinism and local nationalism both exist to a serious extent . . .'

Does this mean that there are occasional outbreaks in the back-country of this enormous China? After all, we are touring only its eastern provinces. In Sinkiang, Mongolia, or Tibet, are there perhaps a few stubborn separatists left? Certainly the problem of nationalities keeps on under every sky and every régime; and it will be fascinating, in the years to come, to study the solutions that Marxist China brings to it. Meanwhile, we had found out how to tease our worthy interpreters: when we were feeling irritable and we had heard some explosion in the distance, we would innocently inquire: 'Is that artillery we hear, firing on some nationalist bourgeois chauvinist uprising?'

Coming back to the Palace of Minorities; the Tibetan room presents the oddest juxtapositions. In one place is recalled for the benefit of visitors the marriage of a Chinese princess of long ago to a lama, with the object of proving the historical links between China and Tibet. Nearby, a photostat of a letter from Lowell Thomas, Jr, to the Lhasa government sets out to establish that American imperialism had its eyes on Tibet.

But what must make more of an impression on Chinese visitors who were starving only yesterday is the showcase displaying a pile of odds and ends found in the dwelling of a wealthy and important Tibetan dignitary who opposed Chinese domination: a bottle of Cognac, a bottle of beer, a cigarette-lighter adorned with a pin-up girl, chocolates, English biscuits, dried shark-fins imported from Hong Kong, a radio, gold coins, and a ceremonial costume. In the high Himalayas, all this evidently suggests unheard-of luxury.

In another place we are shown rather primitive instruments of torture, supposedly used by the bourgeois Tibetan police against the patriots. Quite unintentionally we embarrass our female interpreter by questioning her about the contents of a certain jar. It seems that here, preserved in formalin for the edification of the masses, is the penis of a patriot, cut off by some nationalist bourgeois chauvinist, no doubt.

In the evening, to relax us after all these horrors, they take us to a display by Chinese acrobats. Their skill is incredible. Frenzied stunters spin eight china plates on the ends of eight bamboo rods, while dancing on one foot on a tightrope six feet above the ground.

THURSDAY, 29 SEPTEMBER

In the morning, a visit to what we had taken at first for a reform school for young delinquents.

Hébert decides to sleep in. Yong, the usual harbinger of Mr Hou's anxieties, is sent to him. He offers to rush him to hospital. Hébert manages to cough, and assures him that a little sleep is all he needs to get him back on his feet. Barefaced bourgeois!

The 'Boarding-School for Special Children' occupies a former orphanage that backs onto the courtyards and buildings that used to make up the Catholic cathedral of Peking. We go through attractive gardens, arcades, and cloisters where 205 'special' children are studying or playing. Their ages are from ten to fifteen, and they are divided into nine classes.

The headmistress begins her explanations. 'This school, the only one of its kind to serve the whole of Peking, takes children in at their parents' request; it is for children who are idle, slovenly, dishonest, destructive . . . They are not retarded children. As their bad habits stem from the vestiges of capitalist ideology, we seek to convert them by combining education with production. In this way, bad habits are replaced by activities of positive political and social value.'

The tour is very interesting. As it is morning, the children are in class. They follow with disciplined attention (not letting even our long noses distract them) instruction in all academic subjects, including politics.

Next we visit the workshops where they will spend the afternoon — carpentry for the boys, sewing and lacework for the girls.

As the children redeem themselves by their work and show themselves to be good students, they are allowed to assume responsibilities on various committees — games, assemblies, sanitation, and so on. For instance these committees organize choirs, little-theatre groups, and athletic teams.

We are fascinated by the 'national defence sport'. This consists of military games in which rifles, flags, miniature planes, and telegraphy figure prominently. These games have the obvious advantage of allowing the children to express their aggressiveness, which is considerable, by channelling it into a socially acceptable activity. As time goes on, they are brought to sublimate it in study and culture.

In the afternoon, a cotton-spinning mill. All the machinery is made in China. Out of the ample statistics recited by the manager, we record here those concerned with production: twenty-seven rolls of 400 pounds each — more than 200,000 yards of material a day, produced by a force of 5600 workers, seventy per cent of whom are women.

'Do your workers live in lodgings attached to the plant?'

'Ninety per cent of them do. The unmarried ones sleep in eight-bed dormitories, while families have separate apartments; but seventy per cent of the workers eat in the canteens. It's less expensive and it relieves the wives of the responsibility.'

'And the children?'

'They spend the day in day-nurseries and kindergartens.'

'Are the workers interested in evening courses?'

'Ninety-two per cent of our employees go to them. The majority are doing high-school work — the rest go to technical school.'

'Is this textile plant unionized?'

'The union includes ninety-six per cent of the workers.'

'Tell us how the union is led and how it works.'

'Seventeen elected workers run the union. It has three main functions: firstly, to stimulate emulation and improve production techniques; secondly, to consider questions of welfare and discipline; thirdly, to organize educational and cultural meetings.'

'What about wages?'

'They are regulated by the State in conformity with the Plan, after discussions at worker and management levels.'

'And the right to strike?'

'It's pointless. Production belongs to the State, which means the people, and the workers have no interest in ceasing to produce. What's more, it never happens.'

'All the same, according to this pamphlet,' and Trudeau takes it out of his pocket, 'Mao Tse-tung has said: "In 1956, in certain districts, a small number of workers and students went on strike."'

The question period is in danger of degenerating into discussion. Mr Hou and our interpreter join the game to convince us that the word 'strike' in the text — although it was published in Peking in 1958 — is a faulty translation. We seem to be on the verge of recriminations, whose nature, duration, and cause remain nebulous . . .

Very well. It seems clear they would like a more restful question. Suppose we tour a dormitory? Very tidy bedrooms that suggest a small convent. In one room we put a few questions to a group of laughing girls whom we caught hanging their slips up to dry on a line stretched across the middle of the room.

'Why do you live here and not with your families?'

'We like it. We have a lot of fun together.'

'How much do you earn a month?'

'Fifty-eight yuan [$23.20] on the average.'

'How much does it cost you to live?'

'Rent is thirty centimes [12¢] a month, and we eat in the canteen for less than fifteen yuan [$6] a month. We manage to save thirty to thirty-five yuan [$12 to $14] out of our monthly wages.'

'To buy what, eventually?'

'That, for instance,' says a girl in overalls, showing us some badminton racquets hanging on the wall. 'A bicycle, perhaps . . .'

Some pictures stuck to the wall (dancers, landscapes in colour, Mao . . .) make us think of a title of de Musset's, and we ask pensively: 'What do girls dream about in China?'

'Oh — about their work, naturally.'

The worst of it is, it seems to be true.

Still, we were beginning to understand that the idea of 'work' has different connotations for a Chinese from what it has for

1—(ABOVE) *Our worthy commissar Mr Hou and the ineffable Pi.*

(BELOW) *We are accompanied by a pretty young Chinese, her too-solemn face framed in thick black braids. She is very graceful in her simple cotton print, white with big green polka-dots; the skirt reaches below her knees, in the style of 1947.*

2—The Chinese revolutionaries influence adults, they even give some attention to the old, but it is on the young that they found all their hopes.

3—Pioneers. It is these red-scarfed kids who in twenty years will be the New Men of a country which at that time will have a billion inhabitants.

4—Carpets, all those carpets . . . The whole world is going to be covered with carpet!

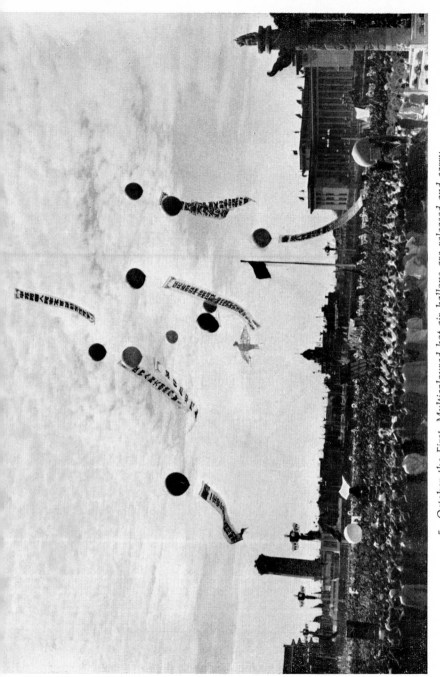

5—October the First. Multicoloured hot-air ballons are released and carry skywards light pennants scribbled over with weighty slogans — reading

6—When we part from him, we salute the monk in the Buddhist manner, putting the hands together at chest level.

7—*Penetrating more than two thousand miles into the interior of China, the Wall is incontestably one of the most extraordinary things we have seen in all our travels.*

Sometimes it is so steep that the Wall is transformed into a gigantic staircase.

the average Occidental. The children whom we asked about their plans for the future insisted on the roles they hoped to play as workers in the society of tomorrow. Dr Lazure has told us how one of the children he questioned never stopped dreaming of becoming a model truckdriver and going to meet Chairman Mao. When we discussed wages and bonuses in the factories, we were assured in the most natural way in the world that the biggest bonus a worker could receive was to be named Hero of Labour.

In Peking prison we had noticed that idleness was outlawed. The prison was like a series of workshops where men and women worked steadily, but without seeming sullen about it. When we were told about the rewards for good conduct, this was synonymous with 'good work'; and bad conduct was punished by isolation — in other words the offender was forbidden to go to work!

Citizens found guilty of minor offences are sent to farms where they become members of 'reform-through-toil teams'; and, as we had seen, difficult children are put in a special school where study and work are equally emphasized.

So it is that, for today's Chinese, work appears as the cardinal virtue, the object of dreams, the universal panacea. And to understand this fully you must recall pre-Communist China, where unspeakable misery and deadly famine were the lot of the unemployed and their whole families. Unemployment meant death by hunger and cold; unemployment, then, was a universal and enduring menace.

And today the revolutionary State has been able to give work to all the Chinese. This means precisely that it has been able to guarantee them the right to live. Before this fundamental fact, all our Western reflections on the arduous nature of work in China, on female labour, on the wretched standard of living, on the totalitarian régime, appear as ineffectual quibbles. In consequence, for any Chinese you talk to, the fact that there is unemployment in the West constitutes the decisive and irrefutable argument against capitalism.

It is through work, then, that the Chinese are recovering their human dignity. And besides, we often noticed, while visiting factories or workshops with some big wheel, that the Chinese worker might be either cheerful and friendly or bored and in-different — but never servile or obsequious. Work was endow-ing him with pride.

This goes so far that people prevented from working by ill-ness — such as those whom we saw at Hangchow Sanatorium — seem bored to death and vaguely uneasy. They aren't used to idleness, and it must bring back old memories of insecurity.

For all that, it would obviously be wrong to conclude that human nature has been transformed in China to the point where arduous labour is one big lark. True, the heads of workshops and directors of communes took pleasure in citing the innumerable poems and popular songs composed to celebrate the glory of labour; but not once did we hear a worker singing — in the fields, in the workshops, in the streets, or at leisure.

Mr Hou speaks to us about the evening's program: French ballet performed by Chinese dancers. The suggestion comes at an un-lucky moment, for we have made up our minds to offer resist-ance to Mr Hou — worthy Mr Hou, likable Mr Hou — who is just a little too rigid as a planner of our tour. '. . . And tomorrow morning we have an appointment with a New Zealand writer.'

'What? But that's impossible,' says Mr Hou, readjusting his hopeless blue cap, which would fall right over his nose if it were not checked by a spirited pair of ears. 'Tomorrow morning, the deputy minister of agriculture is giving an important lecture — '

This will be a test of strength.

10 A few thousand visitors

Vice seeks to conceal itself, but virtue wishes to be seen and known by all. — CONFUCIUS

In pre-Communist China one could meet an improbable assortment of adventurers from all over the world — poets, hobos, pimps, idealists, and soldiers of fortune. These, in the jargon of Canton and Shanghai, were the 'Old China Hands'.

Trudeau, as we have seen, claimed to have been in China in 1949, though he had never succeeded in proving it — after all, it could have been by luck that he discovered those mysterious pagodas and magnificent gardens where he led us in the course of his nocturnal escapades . . . Anyway, Trudeau had heard much of Rewi Alley in those days, and he wanted us to meet him at all costs. This was no ordinary adventurer. A New Zealander who had been settled in China for more than thirty years, he had soon become convinced that the co-operative movement and technical education were essential for the economic liberation of China, and he had organized centres in the most remote districts. After the Communists came to power, he quite naturally continued to live and write in his adopted country.

He is a thickset, red-haired man with an open and friendly look on his face. He greeted us in the traditional manner, by putting his hands together. This beautiful gesture is increasingly rare in China; the revolutionaries, no doubt associating it with the Buddhist greeting, are replacing it with the commonplace handshake.

We take advantage of this meeting mainly to clarify certain points about the Chinese mentality. We ask this man, who knows the country better than anyone else and has a profound affection for the Chinese, to explain, for instance, why everyone

we talk to refuses to admit the least fault, the smallest imper-
fection in the Revolution.

'The Chinese have often had to suffer from the bad faith of
Westerners; when they admit some slight error or failing,
Westerners subsequently exaggerate it to the point of turning
it into a condemnation of the whole system. Hence some natural
reticence in front of potential enemies, whether they are foreigners or even Chinese — because there are still groups in China
who can't stomach the revolution: mullahs, lamas, and their
followings, and also the former wealthy merchants and landed
proprietors.'

'What about the Christians?'

'I know several Christian communities. Those who understand
the situation do their best to vie with the Communists in self-
denial and dedication.'

'Just yesterday, when we visited a former Christian orphanage
converted into a special school, we were told that its French
director had been driven out in 1951 because she had murdered
many children. We used to hear the same about Canadian nuns.
Don't these stories seem incredible to you?'

'You have to look at these problems in context. In the atmosphere of the Old China, life was cheap. The nuns welcomed in
all sorts of abandoned, weak, and diseased children. Their chief
concern was to baptize them, because they often had nowhere
to keep them and no means of bringing them back to health. In
consequence they died in large numbers, and the nuns had to
dispose of many small corpses. Hence these accusations.'

Alley, who is full of anecdotes, has travelled a great deal in
the back-country. He paints us a picture of a China that is de-
veloping prodigiously; that is opening up vast tracts of desert
and swamp to agriculture or mining.

'Precisely because of the size of the task and the loftiness of
the aims, there are very few abuses. Exemplary conduct is
essential for the party members. They even set up opportunities
for the people to criticize them severely when they fall short of
the high ideals they have set themselves.'

Poor Mr Hou. He will certainly be severely criticized for allowing us to meet Rewi Alley instead of dragging us to the

deputy minister of agriculture's lecture. And this on the very eve of the national holiday!

At seven p.m, the great banquet to launch the celebrations of the national day, October the First. There are close to five thousand guests in the great hall of Congress, nearly half of them foreign visitors. What is the explanation of such liberal and unusual hospitality?

Barred from the United Nations, shunned by virtually all non-Communist countries, vilified daily by American propaganda, Red China found itself cut off for a long time from communication with most of the world. China had leprosy.

In the early years of the Revolution, this didn't matter much. There were immediate tasks to be finished, Chiang's stables to be cleaned out, Marxism to be sold to the millions of peasants and bourgeois of the mild Middle Kingdom.

Soon, though, what can only be called the alarming efficiency of the régime transformed the face of China. This new face they were more than willing to show off. 'Come and see,' Chou En-lai had said at the time of the Bandung Conference. But the country was not yet ready to receive an uncontrolled influx of tourists — who for their part were little inclined to visit a remote country, peopled by bloodthirsty Fu Man Chus and destitute of Western embassies.

So the Chinese conceived a magic formula that was bound to make the American-sponsored diplomatic boycott useless. All that was needed was to think of it; now, thousands of foreigners are invited to China every year.

A country doesn't choose the tourists, still less the journalists, who come to see it. But it can choose the people to whom it offers a month of travel with all expenses paid. Costly? Far less so than American propaganda. Three thousand foreigners a year at an average cost to the State of (say) $3000 each, for a total of $9 million. Need one say more?

Every year these foreigners — writers, sociologists, artists, teachers, scholars, trade-unionists, and politicians — will write thousands of articles and books, and will make China known through hundreds of lectures.

Obviously, one would think, the Chinese invite only Communists or people sympathetic to the Chinese Revolution. No. The Chinese are not stupid. They do invite Communists, naturally. While recognizing the USSR (at least in speeches) as the leader of the Communist world, the Chinese feel flattered to see Western Communists go into raptures over their stunning achievements. As for the Eastern Communists, Peking is their godfather — and Moscow had better believe it. When they go back to their own countries, both lots will carry excellent pro-Chinese propaganda to their comrades. The operation may not pay for itself right away, but it is sure to in the near future.

The most numerous visitors, though, seem to be left-wing intellectuals, 'liberal-minded people', decent types in favour of peace, co-existence, the recognition of China — and the Peking Opera. An oddly mixed bag in which you find Simone de Beauvoir rubbing shoulders with a minor Christian-Democrat journalist from Chile, an eminent Australian professor beside a young liberal barrister from Bombay, an English Labour MP and a Catholic writer from Saõ Paulo, a reader of *Esprit*. Whether they become enthusiastic propagandists for Red China or balanced but sympathetic reporters, it is these decent types that form the most profitable contingent.

Finally the Chinese also invite a fair number of right-wingers — bank presidents like James Muir, weight-lifters like Ben Weider, even Conservative MP's like Mr Diefenbaker. These are more cautious people, some of whom will sometimes try to excuse their trips by becoming violent critics of Mao Tse-tung's régime. But even the fiercest, if they are not basically dishonest, will praise some achievements — the ones nobody can miss seeing. These reservations in China's favour are worth their weight in gold, because they reach the readers of *Time* or the Montreal *Gazette* — a public which has never before heard anything good about the régime. In inviting three thousand foreigners, of all shades of opinion, to China every year, the Chinese are betting on a sure thing.

In the vast hall of Congress, then, five thousand guests are talking about China. To make sure that they do, all the important personalities of the régime are distributed among the tables of the foreign delegations. But the leftovers fall to the Canadians: a member of Congress (who belongs to its policy committee), a trade-unionist, a theatrical director, and a pretty but shy woman.

Speech-time is here, and, far away though we are, we do recognize Prime Minister Chou En-lai's eyebrows establishing themselves behind a microphone. The banquet has been abundant, the toasts numerous, the company pleasant. Still, a few fragments of sentences hit our eardrums, loaded with new and original ideas — 'The General Line . . . the Great Leap Forward . . . the people's communes . . . make China a land whose industry, agriculture, science, and culture are modern . . . the unity of the socialist camp led by the Soviet Union . . . the militarism of the imperialist bloc led by the United States . . . friends from Asia, Africa, and Latin America . . .'

No, it's not Bourassa at the Eucharistic Congress. All the same, the Chinese can take pride in their prime minister and his oratorical talents. As Churchill said of Macmillan, 'After all, he's the best prime minister we've got.'

SATURDAY, 1 OCTOBER
The great day: the anniversary of the Revolution, the national holiday.

It must have taken a gigantic organization to coach all the groups of workers, peasants, artists, and students who are going to take part in this morning's mammoth parade. An expert general staff, one imagines, has timed and regulated everything to prevent the unspeakable confusion that would be caused by bottlenecks. In two hours, half a million human beings are to march past the Tien An Men, the colossal red gate of the Forbidden City. Mao Tse-tung is there, on the balcony in front of the great gate, surrounded by dignitaries. We can see him because we are quite close, but the crowd that fills the square has no need to see its god. Enough to know that he is there, that he is watching and applauding.

From the top of our stand we contemplate this moving, many-coloured mass, a field of flowers swaying in the wind. Immense portraits dominate the square: Mao Tse-tung and Sun Yat-sen; Marx, Engels, Lenin, and Stalin.

Ten o'clock strikes. From the far end of the long avenue comes the vanguard of the parade: a group of children — five hundred or a thousand, you can't tell — who at the moment they pass Mao open their small hands to release doves that flutter up into the sky. Some other children let fly a thousand balloons that rush up to play with the doves.

Multicoloured hot-air balloons are released and carry skywards light pennants scribbled over with weighty slogans — reading-matter for American fliers!

Loudspeakers hidden in the monumental streetlamps of the avenue flood all China with joyful music, performed on the spot by the most imposing military band we have ever seen.

Delegations of workers holding high their placards — bearing watchwords, glorious statistics, or graphs showing the latest triumph of some factory, a model of which rides by on a truck. Over and over again, thousands of red flags rise out of the supercharged mass like flames leaping up from a brazier.

Next, marching a hundred abreast, come the little people of the communes — men, women, and children, the youngest in baby-carriages. A float bearing fat pigs, plump sheep, race-horses, cows, chickens, and ducks assures Mao that the commune has heeded his directive to rear livestock.

Other wagons are loaded with gigantic models of wine-bottles, jam-jars, bicycles, and a hundred consumer products now made in China by these ecstatic workers.

Here come the students of the University of Peking, athletic, glowing with health. A delegation of Chinese from overseas, playing accordions. The field of flowers turns yellow, then green, but never fails to revert to red, the colour that has always been the favourite of the Chinese.

More balloons and pennants. We ask Yong to translate the slogans that have just brought a burst of applause from the foreign visitors: 'Emancipation for Africa! Emancipation for Latin America!'

The parade goes on, sometimes covering the broad avenue from one side to the other. How many tens of thousands of

Chinese have marched past us in the last quarter-hour? But that's only the beginning. We see girls, jugglers, swimming champions in bathing-suits, acrobats carrying long rippling silken pennants, peasants flourishing great papier-mâché ears of wheat, dancers swathed in turquoise silk. More balloons — ten linked together to put in orbit a Picasso dove the size of a bus. A giant waterlily carried by hundreds of girls in pink and blue who represent a pond and have great fun being waves. A paper dragon held on the ends of poles by twelve athletes, more flags, more sun beating down on our heads, and they're spinning, spinning . . .

Not a rifle, not the least little tank, not the shadow of a warplane — this is the day of the dove.

We leave the stand like sleepwalkers, stupefied by all that sun, all that fanfare, all that colour, all that shouting, all that mass of humanity now pouring into the street — a few millions, we suppose, out of the six hundred and fifty.

The Yellow Peril? — You said it . . .

Back to the Chen Mein Hotel, feeling starved. We have just started our siesta when Yong arrives with a message. Nobody had remembered to tell us that to mark the occasion the minister of information — or culture, we're not clear which — was giving a cocktail party for foreign journalists. This is interesting, since in spite of all the thousands of foreign visitors in China at this moment such gatherings are rare.

So we spend three hours gorging ourselves on canapés and shaking hands with a few hundred journalists. Many official or unofficial representatives of the young nations of Africa. Now that the euphoria of festivals of liberation has passed, the Africans are worried by the social and economic disarray in which the West has left them. Where are they to seek light and comfort? In the USSR and, more and more, in China, where they are welcomed as brothers. What impresses the African visitors is the dazzling progress China has made in eleven years. Yesterday a backward country exploited by the whites, today China is building blast-furnaces. So you don't *have* to have a white skin to build blast-furnaces?

We meet several South American journalists, also deeply im-

pressed by their visit, and at the same time slightly irritated by
the severity of their 'Mr Hou', who leaves them no more leisure
than ours does us. A nice fat Peruvian poet raises his hands to
heaven and confides: 'It's incredible! We're not allowed five
minutes off. It's almost time to leave and I still haven't had a
chance to buy a dress for my wife. And the most infuriating
thing is, I'm a Communist myself!'

However, the Chinese are making every effort to please the
Latin Americans, who seem to us to be clearly the biggest
foreign contingent this year. Journalists from Mexico, Cuba,
Chile, Peru, and Argentina follow one another to the microphone. In high spirits from the yellow wine, they launch into
incongruous diatribes in which they call God to witness that
China's friendship is going to rescue them one day. Castro's
name figures largely in their flights of oratory, and never fails
to draw thunderous applause.

In the evening, back to the stands in the great square to watch
a colossal firework display: a magical and awesome spectacle
that illumines the whole sky with fountains of light, explosions
of colour, glowing abstractions. From time to time giant rockets
hurl myriads of small luminous parachutes into the sky, to float
gently back to earth from the depths of the night.

The fireworks are let off from some twenty stations spaced
out over a mile and more, yet the synchronization is perfect. The
show goes on for twenty minutes at a stretch, subsides, then
resumes; between times the crowd in the square and in the
streets forms a circle, becomes an orchestra, is transformed into
a corps de ballet; and everything is dancing, is playing, is bustle
and jubilation.

Meanwhile, on top of the Tien An Men gate, the leading
members of the foreign delegations are being entertained.
Tumblers, conjurors, jugglers, and dancers dazzle the guests,
while the prime minister of China, Chou En-lai, moves among
them, chatting with everybody, shaking hands, and gazing
deeply into excited eyes. Twice he gives his hand to the leader
of the Canadian group, but not one word does he breathe about
Mr Diefenbaker — or even René Lévesque.

Next we go, a few at a time, into the great hall, where we meet, one after the other, Liu Shao-chi, president of the Republic; Chu Teh, speaker of Congress; Dong Bei-ou, vice-president of the Republic; and Mao Tse-tung, chairman of the Communist Party. It is a stirring moment: these greybeards, in their ripe old age, embody today the triumph of an idea, an idea that has turned the whole world upside down and profoundly changed the course of human history.

The hubbub of the crowd in the street, the explosions of fireworks in the sky, seem to come from very far away. Here, in the subdued light, the masters of a quarter of mankind wear the mild and peaceful expressions of Buddhas. Mao Tse-tung, one of the great men of the century, has a powerful head, an unlined face, and a look of wisdom tinged with melancholy. The eyes in that tranquil face are heavy with having seen too much of the misery of men.

At 10.30 Mr Hou is shepherding his little flock back to the hotel. 'Tonight the crowd will be too dense and excited,' he says; 'you would be dangerously jostled.' But the Leader of the Canadian group swears to himself that he will have none of that. What? The Chinese Fourteenth of July, and he is not to storm the Bastille?

As the party leaves the Tien An Men gate, Trudeau hides for a moment behind a pillar, then darts towards the crowd that is swirling round the square. In an instant he is caught up, sucked in, and swallowed by the maelstrom of people, and lost to Mr Hou.

What happened after that we shall never know exactly, nor are we convinced that Trudeau remembers it clearly himself. He took part in weird and frenzied dances, in impromptu skits, in delightful flirtations; he described exotic orchestras, costumes of the moon-people, strange friendships, and new scents; he told of jackets of (imitation) leather, dark tresses, inquisitive children, laughing adolescents, brotherly and joyful men. Then he spoke of a weariness that imperceptibly settled on the city along with the dust, no longer kicked up by millions of dancing feet; he spoke too of lights being extinguished, voices growing hoarse,

dances that gradually lost their speed and groups that grew
steadily smaller; of trucks filled with soldiers at the end of their
leaves, of busloads of departing peasants, of small parties strag-
gling along the streets, of light footsteps in deserted alleyways,
of dark lanterns, of the end of the masquerade; and of a very
long walk through a sleeping capital in the small hours of the
morning.

Having stealthily entered the hotel, our Leader steps into a
hot bath. Just as he is congratulating himself on his incognito
escapade, there is a knock on the door.

Trudeau opens the door a crack and perceives the stern visage
of Mr Hou, and Mr Wen himself, vice-president of the Chinese
People's Association for Cultural Relations with Foreign Countries. Out of deference for this important dignitary, the bather
puts on his underpants and invites the gentlemen to come in.

A conversation in gestures ensues, but doesn't get very far.
At last Trudeau understands that he is supposed to put his
trousers on. But just as he becomes convinced that he is going
to be sent to Mongolia, Mr Wen introduces a magnificent young
woman, thoroughly intimidated. So that's it! — she is the only
interpreter they could dig up at this late hour.

In impeccable French, the girl translates Mr Wen's anxious
reproaches. 'You could have got lost or had an accident, walking
all by yourself at night.'

Trudeau can no longer resist teasing: 'Clearly I would have
felt less lonely with a pretty girl like you at my side.' But the
interpreter is impervious to this kind of thing, and translates to
Mr Wen the compliments intended for her. Misunderstanding
spreads, confusion becomes universal, the Plan is destroyed, the
General Line takes on peculiar aspects, and Trudeau speaks of a
Great Leap Forward to his tub. Decidedly this is not the night
for building socialism.

11 Industry and culture in the service of the State

Better an imperfect diamond than a perfect pebble.

— CONFUCIUS

In the morning we are taken to an 'important lecture on industry' given by Chueh Mu-chiao, vice-chairman of the Planning Board.

In 1949 the number of factory and office workers employed in Chinese industry was only three million. In 1960 the figure had risen to twenty million. Mr Chueh wants to describe for us the three stages of this industrialization.

From 1949 to 1952 the concentration was on putting back on its feet an economy shattered by eight years of war against the Japanese and four against the Kuomintang. Annual production increased by thirty-four per cent.

From 1953 to 1957 the first Five Year Plan laid the foundations of industrialization and transformed agriculture. First the socialist State took over those industries that had belonged to the State under Chiang. Next the capitalist enterprises of the nation were gradually transformed so that the Chinese capitalists became first co-owners and then rentiers. Finally cottage industries were organized in co-operatives, before becoming the property of local governments. The average increase in production during the first Five Year Plan was eighteen per cent.

The period 1958 to 1963 is that of the Great Leap Forward, with the second Five Year Plan. Socialism is well and truly launched, and already annual production is increasing at a rate of fifty-two per cent.

For the rest of his lecture Mr Chueh buries us in production statistics. The Latin Americans follow him the way horse-players at a track follow a jockey, and they burst into applause as China finishes in the money among the industrial nations.

Those interested will find these figures in the official publications; other readers will thank us to quote as few as possible. For, were we inclined to attach much importance to statistics, this book would look like a set of logarithmic tables. In fact everyone who spoke to us, at each meeting, pelted us with figures; and in a general way we distrust them. Not that we took our informants for liars. But they were generally incapable of bringing out the significance of a statistic, by comparisons, for instance. It's not much use knowing that a machine produces ten whatsits a second if you have no facts to compare this performance with.

By contrast the question of the standard of living interests everybody. And the attentive traveller — if he noses about the shop windows and questions plenty of people — can collect enough information to throw some little light on the matter. So here is a summary of the facts we collected. By assembling them in a few paragraphs, we will spare ourselves from cluttering the rest of the book with them.

The highest salary we heard of was paid to Mr Lieu, a former capitalist now managing a large enterprise: 500 yuan a month ($200). A leading movie star, Being-Yang of the Shanghai studios, reached 330 yuan ($132) a month if she made enough films.

A young graduate in medicine earns 56 yuan ($22.40) a month, but after two or three years in practice, if he is competent and his ideological attitude is healthy, he reaches 100 yuan ($40).

In heavy industry (railway cars, automobiles, machine tools, blast-furnaces), wages are scaled through eight categories, from 33 yuan ($13.20) to 105 ($42) a month. By comparison, in light and cottage industries (carpetmaking, for instance), the scale is from 30 to 76 yuan ($12 to $30.40) a month. A twenty-four-year-old weaver earned 70 yuan a month ($28), the same as our driver in Peking.

Taking into account premiums for high production in piece-work, occasional distributions of products in consumer-goods factories, and bonuses for exceeding planned quotas, industrial wages can reach a maximum of 150 yuan ($60) a month.

As for agricultural wages, they are much lower. In rural communes near Peking, Shanghai, and Canton, we found an average family income of about 530 yuan a year ($212); that is to say, the principal wage-earner might get between 20 and 30 yuan a month ($8 to $12), his wife and the old people less. But it must be added that agricultural workers have the right to eke out their incomes by raising some stock or crops on their own; also, the members of the commune get their basic diet free. In some communes they are given a pound of rice per person per day, plus occasional allowances of sugar, vegetables, and fish; meat is given out free only on public holidays, that is five or six times a year.

What do these incomes mean in terms of purchasing power? It is almost meaningless to know that in China we exchanged our dollars at the rate of 42.6¢ for a yuan, and that in Moscow the yuan was worth only about eight cents. (For simplicity, the calculations in this book are based on 40¢ to the yuan.) It is more significant to look at the purchasing power of the yuan for the Chinese worker. We are told that a Chinese can live on twelve yuan a month, that is, $4.80. But, so that the reader may judge for himself, here are a few prices.

Essentials like rice and cotton are cheap, but they are rationed so that nobody will get more than his fair share. A large bowl of steamed rice sold for .05 yuan (2¢) in the canteen. Rents are also relatively low: the automotive workers of Changchun were housed in modern apartments where they paid 4.4 yuan a month ($1.76) for three furnished rooms plus a toilet. In a suburb of Shanghai, the same arrangement cost twice as much. In these apartments water and electricity are supplied for ten centimes (4¢) a month per family; heating is free. For the unmarried, many factories have dormitories, where it costs .30 yuan (12¢) a month to share a room with five other people. (It goes without saying that at the present moment an infinitesimal fraction of the Chinese can leave their slums to live in these phalansteries and dormitories. The selection is made by the 'street committee' according to criteria that we never managed to pin down exactly — value of work, kind of job, distance from the factory, size of family, and so on.)

The State pays half the price of medicines, and supplies free medical care and free working clothes. Workers have two weeks' holiday with pay a year, plus three days' leave for the celebrations of the First of October, two for May Day, three for the Spring Festival — in principle!

Admission to the art museum was .05 yuan (2¢), to the 'Grand Monde' recreational centre .25 yuan (10¢). Cloth shoes sold for 4 yuan ($1.60), leather ones for 23 ($9.20). Pickles retailed at .80 a jar (32¢), perfumed soaps at 1 yuan (40¢). The price of a cotton shirt was 10 yuan ($4), of a coarse wool sweater 30 yuan ($12). Finally, you can have a three-speed record player for 180 yuan ($72).

Oof! perhaps that will do for the moment. We must hurry back to the hotel and have a heart-to-heart talk with Mr Hou . . .

Even though we are the guests of China, we don't take kindly to being led about by the hand like small children *all* the time. We demand just a little time off on occasion, whether to make our own observations or to get a chance to put our observations in writing; in short, we demand that Mr Hou should allow us a little of that Peace he talks about so much.

After these representations, and last night's scene in Trudeau's room, Mr. Hou and Kao — disappear. Actually, it was natural that the latter should be sent back to the Institute of Foreign Languages after missing almost two weeks' lectures on our account. But what have they done with Mr. Hou? Already remorse begins to gnaw at us. We picture him being re-educated by shovelling coal in some mine in the north-east! Really we were very fond of good old Hou after all. We'll miss him.

There is a knock at our door. It's a girl named Pei, an English-language interpreter, followed shyly by Yong. 'What would you say to a visit to the historical museum?'

Yes, that interests us. She hands each of us a piece of paper with a few ideograms on it. 'That means: "I am a member of a group of visiting Canadians. Please be kind enough to guide

me back to the Chen Mein Hotel." ' Our visas for liberty! 'With
that,' adds Pei with a smile, 'if you lose your way during a stroll
in Peking, somebody will bring you back.'

The curator of the museum, whom Pei had warned by telephone, is waiting for us at the door of the imposing building,
constructed and fitted out in less than a year as part of the
Great Leap Forward. He is a very well-bred, very mandarin old
gentleman. 'As Confucius said,' he begins, 'when friends have
come from far away, we are happy.'

He is the first Chinese to quote Confucius to us.

We start, of course, with tea in the curator's room, which is
furnished in exquisite taste: Cantonese armchairs, lacquered
screens from Foukien, carved tables from Shantung. After tea,
our host insists on taking us round the museum himself.

Here they have done their best to cook history in Marxist
sauce. The idea was to illustrate the revolutionary tradition of
the Chinese people, a theme dear to the heart of Mao Tse-tung,
who has written somewhere: 'Throughout the thousands of years
of Han history, there have been hundreds of peasants' revolts,
large or small, against the obscurantist régime imposed by the
great landowners and the nobility.'

'We have followed the directives of Chairman Mao,' says the
curator.

They have divided the museum — that is to say the history
of China — into three parts: primitive society, going back
500,000 years with Peking Man and ending about 4000 years
ago; slave society, from 2000 to 475 B.C.; feudal society, which
ended in A.D. 1840.

We don't linger over the fossilized skulls, the jawbone of
Changyang Man, or the spearheads, which offer little scope for
the really quite subtle propaganda that our venerable guide
insinuates between his purely historical remarks.

In the galleries devoted to the 'slave society', it's much easier.
The exposition ends with: 'The oppression and exploitation
indulged in by the slaveholders gave rise to resistance and un-
ceasing struggles on the part of the slaves and craftsmen which
precipitated the disintegration of the system.'

The last series of galleries, illustrating a glorious epoch in the history of China, stresses the hatefulness of the feudal system and the nobility to the peasants, whose revolts invariably overcame emperors who were too despotic. It was recognized, all the same, that one emperor granted more rights to the people, that another contributed to the unification of China, or to winning the minorities over.

Even though the museum closed an hour ago, the curator won't let us leave before we have had a little more tea, given our opinion and 'advice', and written 'something' in the golden book. Then — a mark of high consideration in China — he sees us to our car.

And to end this already full day Pei takes us to see *Swan Lake*, danced by Chinese; for in seven years they have mastered Western classical ballet. 'Soviet experts helped us,' says Pei modestly.

U Nu, prime minister of Burma, is at the performance, attended by a suite of pretty girls in Burmese national costumes. He gets far more applause than the dancers.

Back to the hotel by bus with a cheerful group of Argentines. They are enjoying their tour of China, except for one bitter disappointment: 'But there's no dancing in this country, and absolutely not a single solitary bar! You could die of boredom here.' Of all the foreign visitors, the Latin Americans clearly suffer most from the epidemic of morality that has been raging in China since this régime came to power. No pubs, no brothels, no dancing, no night-clubs, nothing but films and shows that, on the moral plane, would delight the hearts of the Board of Censors of the Province of Quebec.

The women of China, with their radiant yet cool charm, as modestly dressed as the Grey Nuns, would never tolerate the smallest attention from a foreigner. One wonders what would happen to a foreigner who dared to offer gallantries to a lady interpreter. (Except on the night of October the First . . .)

A young South American, on the verge of a nervous breakdown, summed the situation up in these terms: *'Son tan morales que desmoralisan!'*

At the Chen Mein Hotel, that dismal boarding-school, everyone has been asleep since nine o'clock, along with all Mao's China.

MONDAY, 3 OCTOBER

This morning a great gathering of all the foreigners who are still in Peking: the deputy minister of culture of the People's Republic of China has something to impart to us, after which he will let us ask him questions.

Groups cluster round the different interpreters — French, English, Spanish, German, Japanese. Simultaneous translation: we can hear all the interpreters simultaneously!

The deputy minister's long speech is not so much about culture as about imperialism, the bourgeoisie, the Americans, Korea, Taiwan, and the Revolution. It lasts a good hour; here are some extracts.

'Old China was eighty per cent illiterate — only twenty per cent of the school-age children went to school. The people suffered numerous diseases — "Asiatic diseases", the Europeans called them. Prostitution, opium, gambling — all the vices were prevalent in the country. After the Revolution everything changed; there was a real change of heart.'

There follows an accusation against 'cultural imperialism': 'The characteristic of our culture is anti-imperialism. The cause of Chinese culture is in the proletariat's hands, no longer in the hands of the bourgeoisie. There may still be some bourgeois intellectuals who propagate bourgeois pacifism and hypocritical humanism, and spread the bourgeois concepts of peaceful evolution. But we have struggled against all that for ten years. The aim of the cultural revolution is to eliminate all differences between intellectuals and workers.

'We have organized a teaching corps of seven million professionals and thirty million amateurs. Education must lead the struggle against imperialism and build socialism by forming socialist consciousness. We have taken over the religious schools created by the imperialists — 21 colleges, 500 secondary schools, and 1100 elementary schools — and they have undergone a complete transformation.'

On adult education: 'There are 39 million workers and peasants learning to read, thanks to evening classes; there are 76 million adults who, having learned to read, are taking more advanced evening courses. Twenty million of these workers and peasants have gone on to the level of higher education.'

On the education of children and adolescents, here are the official facts:

Children in kindergarten	21,000,000
Before the Revolution	130,000
Children in elementary schools	90,000,000
Before the Revolution	23,000,000
Children in secondary schools	12,900,000
Before the Revolution	1,800,000
Students in universities	810,000
Before the Revolution	155,000

In connection with these last figures, it is pointed out to us that since the Liberation half a million Chinese have graduated from universities, compared with a quarter of a million in the preceding half-century.

Nevertheless, the privileges formerly enjoyed by the bourgeois classes still leave their traces: 'Children of workers and peasants today constitute ninety per cent of the enrolment in the elementary schools, eighty per cent in the secondary schools, and only fifty per cent in institutions of higher learning.'

The millions of Chinese who can now read and write thanks to Mao seem to be grateful to him, as witness this popular song, apparently written by a grateful worker or peasant:

> *Yesterday I was freed from illiteracy,*
> *So today I start to write fearlessly.*
> *The first phrase I write is 'Chairman Mao',*
> *The second is 'the Communist Party'.*
> *I write nothing for the third phrase,*
> *But draw a sunflower facing the sun.*

After the deputy minister's long speech, there is a question period in which the answers are given by less important officials. They are never discountenanced, though the questioning is sometimes aggressive.

A LUXEMBURGER: 'Is it fair to speak of imperialism in connection with the schools that foreign countries had set up in China?'

ANSWER: 'These religious schools were chiefly subsidized by the American imperialists. In fact, the United States subsidized eighteen of the twenty-one colleges and 255 secondary schools.'

THE LUXEMBURGER: 'Books are the precious links between different cultures. By what criteria do you ban foreign books in China?'

ANSWER: 'We ban books hostile to Communism and to China, books that praise the American way of life — and, naturally, erotic books.'

A MOROCCAN: 'Is elementary education compulsory?'

ANSWER: 'You can't call it compulsory, but almost all Chinese children go to school. In some districts there are still children who don't, for want of places.'

A BRAZILIAN: 'What foreign films are distributed in China?'

ANSWER: 'After the Liberation, imperialist culture was abolished as a demoralizing influence that weakened the national struggle. But we welcome progressive foreign films with pleasure. Just now *La Traviata* is being shown.'

But long before the end of the question period two Canadians have slipped away to sun themselves. These group exercises remind us too much of our college days when disingenuous professors used to reduce all the facts to the highest common denominator of Thomism. And decidedly, when we are trying to get to the heart of a matter, we don't like being preached at all the time.

Never mind, we're going to have dinner with our friend McIntosh — he always has a dozen stories for us. He's a great admirer of Groucho Marx, and quotes him without a pause between two lines of Shakespeare. The latest one is: 'I wouldn't be a member of a club that would have me as a member.'

We must say goodbye; we are leaving for Shanghai tomorrow, and McIntosh doesn't know yet what his itinerary is to be.

12 Shanghai revisited

Those who would be unchangingly happy or wise must change often. — CONFUCIUS

Towards eight o'clock in the morning we get on the Shanghai train, which will be our home for twenty-six hours. What's more, it's a sort of express, stopping only in the main cities. The distance is about 900 miles.

Comfortable compartments, with four berths. On a small table there are some large teacups, a lamp, and a foliage plant. Every now and then an employee with a huge thermos comes in and fills the cups, free. But it's only in the stations that one can buy fruit (very expensive) and candies at absolutely prohibitive prices. How on earth can the Chinese pay three dollars a pound for toffee? But they buy it. Mr Hou watches them blankly. . . . No, Mr Hou *wasn't* sent to the coal mines! He will be with us to the end, but it's clear that he has been asked to shut his eyes to some of the eccentricities of the bourgeois Canadians entrusted to his care.

On the other hand, we have lost both Kao and Yong, who are replaced by another student from the Institute of Foreign Languages. A young man dressed all in black, whom we instantly christen 'Frère Untel' — thereby doing a grave injustice to the real Frère Untel, who is in fact not a bit like the ineffable Pi.

Like his predecessors, Pi is a zealous, devoted, and charming interpreter. But — whether it is our *joual* that confuses him or our irreverence that puts him off — he gets into serious difficulties whenever he has to translate the remarks of our Chinese friends into French.

For instance, he confuses certain like-sounding words. When he tells us that, 'after being sanctioned, the imperial looked at itself in the cupboard and committed suicide according to costume,' we must understand that, 'after being sentenced, the empress looked at herself in the mirror and was executed according to custom.' Well, we'll get used to it. It's harder to get used to this endless journey, whose only events are meals.

At lunch we are served sea-slugs, a delicacy the Chinese have a passion for. This is a quite repulsive beast which lives in slime and looks like a fat, brownish worm covered with bumps — whether they are tentacles or just warts, we don't know. The creature is about six inches long and an inch in diameter. It has no taste, but the Chinese insist that its rubbery flesh is pleasant to munch.

The group has conspired to tell our hosts that Trudeau adores sea-slugs, which is a slight exaggeration. He will be served them to the day of our departure!

Four coaches (with hard benches) separate us from the dining-car. They are full to overflowing; soldiers and civilians, simply dressed, clean, and smiling, play cards or chess or read Chinese comic-books — which are unlike American comic-books in being compulsively moral: official propaganda chopped up into candies for children of all ages. Loudspeakers flood the train with great airs from opera — Peking Opera, that is.

We meet employees armed with fly-swatters (just in case!) and dusters. As the dust and soot settles over everything, they keep raising it again; and they spray the first-class compartments with perfume. Just before Shanghai, the conductor will ask us if we have had a pleasant journey: 'Are you satisfied with the cleanliness — the cuisine — the service? I beg you to give us advice, for we have not had much experience yet.' Is it on orders, or is it just Chinese politeness?

During the night we cross the Blue River (Yangtze Kiang) on a train-ferry; but the operation is carried out so unobtrusively that most of the passengers are unaware of it. Trudeau is awakened, however, and decides to go outside to watch the transshipment — and see if the river is really blue. Normally that would have been bound to alarm Mr Hou. But our worthy commissar just opens one eye and shuts it again as if he had seen nothing. The conductor feels differently. He runs after Trudeau and explains to him — with the help of a Chinese

interpreter, hurriedly awakened, who knows a little German! —
that his life is in danger. Suiting the action to the *verboten*, he
grabs Trudeau by the sleeve and takes him back to the train.
Such an attitude is explained by the obsession the Chinese have
that some misfortune might happen to one of their guests. And
one does understand that the conductor would hardly like to
'confess' to the comrades, at the next self-criticism session, that
he let a Canadian drown himself in the approaches to Nanking
harbour.

WEDNESDAY, 5 OCTOBER

For the past hour Mr Hou has been telling us that we arrive in
Shanghai in ten minutes. Time to say our farewells to our
fellow-passengers: a Swedish architect, a Norwegian economist,
a woman doctor who runs a children's hospital in Reykjavik, an
Australian dentist, and an ill-defined gentleman who might be
a fake Belgian count.

On the station platform, an imposing reception committee is
awaiting us. 'This is the best-known doctor of Shanghai,' says
Pi, introducing a little man in blue denims whom we had taken
for a porter. 'This is the best-known economist of Shanghai,
this is the best-known journalist of Shanghai, this is the leader
of the biggest textile union . . .'

Two Soviet-made cars take us to the Peace Hotel, the former
Cathay, which was the pride of the British in the 'golden age'
of imperialism and the international concessions. In front of it
we recognize the little park where English nurses used to walk
their pink-cheeked charges. The only thing missing is the sign
at the gate that used to say 'No Chinese or dogs allowed'.

At one o'clock we have tea with the local representative of
the Cultural Association, a cultivated and charming man. He
wants to know what *we* would like to find out about Shanghai
— the largest city in China with its ten million inhabitants, the
great centre of culture and commerce, the cradle of the Chinese
Communist Party.

A tour of the city. On the balcony of a skyscraper they point out to us, not without a touch of malice, the former divisions: 'This used to be the French concession; over there, the British; beyond the bridge, the Japanese quarter.'

Trudeau finds it strange to come back after eleven years to a city that used to embody all the fascination, all the intrigue, all the violence and mystery that could arise from the collision of East and West. He had left behind him a busy port, a metropolis in disorder but not in panic, its sidewalks full of beggars and wounded soldiers; a place where the businessmen were divided between haste to liquidate everything and fear of finding themselves stuck with a worthless currency.

The city is still lively, and on the whole its appearance has changed little. Certainly the streets are cleaner, and among the dense crowds that pour into the streets every day you now see hardly anybody in rags.

European travellers still give enthusiastic descriptions of Shanghai, astonishing to the North American, who can't get excited over turn-of-the-century skyscrapers. In fact the really curious thing is the sense of watching a Communist play being performed in front of a pretentious and dreary capitalist back-drop. Fifteen-storey bank buildings, whose useless Doric columns bear witness to the bad taste of English businessmen, now house the industrious servants of the Chinese State. The monograms of the 'golden age' have been erased from the façades; the fore-heads of these stone or reinforced-concrete cyclopes are all marked with the same great red star.

In this city, once both the pride and the shame of the whites, we haven't seen a single foreigner, except at the hotel — but it is intended for visitors of our kind. Not long ago Shanghai still had a few refuges for Westerners homesick for jazz and Scotch. Now our nocturnal escapades don't uncover a single one.

In the evening we are taken to the former Orient Hotel, in other days 'a capitalist gambling den and place of amusement', which 'after the Liberation' became a workers' cultural centre, a 'palace of culture'. There must be eighteen of these in Shang-hai, not to mention some 1600 small cultural centres attached to factories.

The director of the palace doesn't conceal from us that in addition to cultural activity properly so called (art shows, folk-lore, little-theatre groups, orchestras), there are plenty of 'courses in Marxism-Leninism', lectures by 'party members', discussions of 'the line', meetings to 'encourage the reading of the works of Mao', and so on. 'Eight thousand workers come to the palace every day,' our host tells us.

It is easy to understand the interest of the Communist Party in an operation like this; but as we tour exhibitions of amateur painting and watch young workers reciting classical plays or rehearsing a concerto, we acknowledge that culture in the true sense has its place here.

We watch a colour film — the life of Gne Re, a young Com-munist patriot, the composer of the Chinese national anthem, who died in 1936 at the age of twenty-four. The acting is stagy and the propaganda heavy-handed, but the music is pleasant and the colours are lovely. It's like watching one of the first 'talkies'.

As we return to the hotel at 10.30 p.m., we go through streets deserted except for a few rare pedicabs, which have replaced the wretched coolies of other days. Shanghai has become an industrious city, and it retires early. At eleven, escaping the vigilance of Mr Hou, we slip surreptitiously out of the hotel and plunge into the heart of what used to be called 'the Chinese city'.

We are fated to return empty-handed from this quest for adventure. The occasional pedestrian eyes us with an air that is hard to define; in the darkness, we don't know if it is dis-turbed — or disturbing. A few times we notice a thread of yellowish light filtering mysteriously into the street and approach the spot; but behind the nearly closed shutters all we find is a few workers having their soup in a greasy-spoon joint before going on the night shift.

But as a ramble, it's marvellous. Sometimes helped by the full moon that manages to penetrate this labyrinth of narrow lanes, we emerge after a seemingly endless walk on a pond bathed in golden light. And a zigzag bridge leads us to an exquisite little pagoda.

THURSDAY, 6 OCTOBER

In spring every confectioner in Canada installs in the middle of his window display one of those gigantic and intricate white wedding-cakes, encumbered with colonnades and wreaths of sugar swarming up to the top storey, where a plaster bride and groom are enthroned: except for the last detail, this is a fair description of the exhibition palace that the Soviets have presented to the people of Shanghai — who don't dare think it ugly. It approaches the architectural folly of the golden age of imperialism, the Victorian era.

Apart from that, the industrial exhibition housed in this 'palace of Sino-Soviet friendship' is substantial, and makes a strong impression on heretics like us. It is hard to believe that in ten years China has been industrialized to the point of being able to export such a variety of products, running the gamut from heavy machinery to ballpoints, by way of the most complex electronic equipment, chemical products, fabrics, musical instruments, motors, toys, machine tools, fine confectioneries, and so on. Even if many of these objects were produced only as prototypes or in very small quantities (and it wouldn't do to exaggerate this possibility, since we have seen foreign importers placing orders), this exhibition gives food for serious thought. It's the same as with the atomic bomb; it's the first one that counts. After that, the capacity is proved.

Pi shows us next a 'craftsmanship salon', which is simply a workshop where all kinds of craftsmen are assembled, from the inevitable gentleman who devotes his life to engraving landscapes or poems by Mao on pieces of ivory the thickness of a grain of rice to the artist who, in less time than it takes to describe it, transforms coloured paper into flowers. In the needlework corner, patient young women faithfully reproduce the washed-out tones of poor colour reproductions clipped from popular magazines. An old man is making improbable ships and dragons out of brass wire and silk. Pi has much trouble explaining to us that some young women are making 'artificial flowers in natural silk that look natural'. 'But are they, in a word, artificial or natural?'

He can't work it out, and we pass on to another old man who, with extraordinary skill, is transforming ordinary dough into figurines of disquietingly bad taste. 'Since the Liberation,' he tells us, 'I have worked steadily, and I am paid by the State. *Before*, the reactionaries prevented me . . .' No doubt these reactionaries had their reasons for not encouraging this confectioner, whose works are not even edible.

Our general impression is that the planners seem to make no distinction between genuine craftsmanship, so abundant and varied in China, and the cheap and nasty.

In the afternoon we tour an old slum district called Ya Sue Lung — which means, according to Pi, 'the little street of medicinal water'. Mr Li, the 'district leader', gives us tea in a modest hut. 'Before the Liberation,' he tells us, 'the twenty thousand people here lived in utter wretchedness. Many were unemployed and nobody had enough to eat. Seventy-five per cent lived in huts, some in tents. They were constantly threatened by three plagues: the rain that seeped into the huts and turned the street into a river of mud; fire, which was very common because of the oil lamps (between 1942 and 1946 there were three fires that destroyed over a thousand hovels); and gales that carried off roofs and even whole dwellings. There were no sewers, no garbage collections, no public fountains. Disease was spread by innumerable flies. Ninety per cent of the inhabitants were illiterate.'

Next, Mr Li takes us on a tour of the district, which the State is improving until it can move all these people to the modern districts that are springing up all round Shanghai. The children follow us in cheerful bands and never tire of clapping us. But the grown-ups — especially the old — give us only unfriendly stares.

They are the same old slums, but they are clean and they have electricity; most of the thatched roofs have been replaced by tiles, the streets are paved, the children are shining with health, the district is watered by thirty-five public fountains, and sewers have been put in everywhere.

When we go back to the district leader's office, we are shown several diplomas the district has been awarded for campaigns against flies, mosquitos, rats, cockroaches, and other dumb chums. 'May I recite a poem that is very popular just now?' asks Mr Li.

> *We eat rice*
> *And we live under a tile roof;*
> *We have social security*
> *And the children go to school;*
> *The streets are clean and we have electric light.*
> *Let us give thanks to the party*
> *And Chairman Mao.*
> *It is the new life,*
> *Thanks to the definition of the General Line*
> *And the Great Leap Forward.*

Yes. Still, it remains possible to like Aragon better.

To show us the future in store for the dwellers in 'the little street of medicinal water', we are taken abruptly into a new district of the suburb, which houses some of the 36,000 workers in the new suburban factories. ('*Before*, there were only four factories and 2300 workers; they had to live right in Shanghai, which meant spending three or four hours a day in buses.')

Construction started in this district in 1959, and already it includes sixty-eight buildings from three to five storeys high, in which 1508 families — 'those who used to live farthest away' — had been housed at first. These buildings, of a vaguely Scandinavian inspiration, are among the pleasantest we have seen in China so far.

'This evening,' announces Pi (that is, as always, Hou via Pi), 'we are going to see Le Grand Meaulnes.' He means, of course, the Grand Monde, once a gaming-house and place of debauchery famous throughout the Orient as the meeting-place of the demi-monde and the underworld. Since the régime decided to purge China of all capitalist vices, the Grand Monde has undergone a radical transformation. Today it is a recreation centre 'for the whole family'.

A stout person (perhaps the former owner 're-educated'? He

has the figure for it!) welcomes us in the street, according to the Chinese custom. The curious and complicated building, all wings and staircases and balconies, has perhaps four or five storeys, it's hard to tell. You keep emerging on an inner court-yard with an open-air stage and a crowd of devotees of acro-batics, balancing acts, and magicians. The special feature of the Grand Monde is that in its various halls it can present simul-taneously three or four operas and as many plays, films, recitals, and concerts. Behind these it has rooms for cards, chess, and ping-pong, and a rifle-range. And then there are restaurants and cafés. You can go in at noon for the moderate sum of .25 yuan (10¢) and watch as many shows as you like up to 10.30 in the evening. There are usually ten thousand people in the establish-ment at once. You go from one opera to another till you find one to your liking. You leave one theatre to catch some good acrobatic act, and then come back to the play. The whole family comes, leaving Grandfather at the opera and picking him up later in the chess room, carrying sleeping babies (who don't seem to be disturbed by clashing cymbals), and enjoying them-selves steadily for hours and hours.

Back at the hotel, after wishing Mr Hou and Pi pleasant dreams, we feel the urge yet again to go for a walk in the city. The banks of the Hwang-Po are beckoning us. To be in Shanghai and not stroll along the waterfront by night . . .

Once we are sure that Mr Hou has gone to bed, we slip discreetly out like students leaving a boarding school without permission. No, that's an exaggeration; Mr Hou has become the most broadminded of prefects.

Eleven o'clock. The city seems dead. There are no bars, of course, but we would have thought we could find a café, a teahouse . . . Still, in a park we notice that imperialism has left more of a mark on this city than on others: several young couples have their arms round each other's waists and are kissing.

13 A factory, a commune, and a capitalist

Does not the desire to avert the inevitable increase one's grief? — CHUANG TZU

A textile factory is on today's program. We've seen *so* many machines already! Tactfully but firmly, we explain to Mrs Ting, the directress, who was prepared to give us a detailed tour of her impressive factory, that we only want to know about the workers' lives, the social organization of the spinning-mill. The Chinese with us are taken aback. Every tour ought to proceed according to a plan determined in advance; any alteration seems out of the question to those conscientious bureaucrats, our hosts.

Mrs Ting doesn't want to lose face. 'That's a pity,' she says. 'This is one of the most modern spinning-mills in China. We have 2120 looms, 68,563 spindles — '

'What would interest us would be to tour only the social services — day-nurseries, restaurants, infirmaries — '

'Since the Liberation, we have increased our production by 285 per cent . . . We have 5300 workers — ' Mrs Ting yields; and, perhaps with regret, but smiling still, she agrees not to talk production.

She pours good green tea in cups the size of beer steins. Incense is burning in one corner of the small room, which is oddly like the parlour of a convent. Coils of blue smoke caress the inevitable photograph of Mao, which is surrounded by red banners adorned with slogans in gold letters. In one corner, on a pedestal, is the traditional fern of our convents.

Mrs Ting, a mother superior in blue denim, adjusts her glasses and awaits our questions resolutely.

'Are there many women among the 5300 workers?'

'About seventy per cent.'

'What happens when one of them becomes pregnant?'

'She works, but after five months she has one paid hour of rest during the working day. From the moment of the delivery, she is given fifty-six days' leave with pay. When she comes back to the factory, she can nurse her child at fixed times, in a special room. The rest of the time the children are under the care of trained nurses in the factory day-nursery, which has 244 beds used by 732 children (in three shifts). Until the baby is eighteen months old, the mother brings it to the day-nursery and takes it home after work.'

'Is it easy for the workers to get an education?'

'Three thousand of them are taking courses. In the factory itself we have an elementary school, a secondary school, and an "evening university". There are no illiterates in this plant. Many of our workers are taking specialized courses. Twenty of them have become mechanical engineers. There is even one well-known writer who was trained here. Because of his special talent, he left the factory and took up journalism.'

'Is there a pension fund?'

'The old receive sixty per cent of their pay after retirement.'

'What about leisure?'

'It is well organized. Depending on their tastes, the workers join choirs, dancing groups, operatic or theatrical companies. They write their own plays.'

'What are the most popular subjects?'

'The production situation, the success of one or other of the working teams, the spirit of the workers — '

'Have you got choreographers too?'

'Of course. One of our workers composed a very fine ballet to explain a good method of running the weaving looms.'

For ten years both the amateurs and the professionals of 'People's Art' in China have had to express only official sentiments, portray only élite workers or brave soldiers on the stage, paint only patriotic pictures. There is no sign of a Pasternak on the horizon . . .

Mrs Ting shows us the factory restaurant — immense, clean, and austere. Hundreds of workers are chatting happily over bowls of rice and plates of meat and vegetables, which cost virtually nothing. The restaurant's monthly statement of revenues and expenditures is affixed to the wall: everybody knows that rice could not be sold more cheaply without causing a deficit.

We visit one of the factory's three medical centres. 'Each worker is entitled to an annual medical examination,' the doctor tells us. 'Besides that, I am concentrating particularly on the detection of cases of cancer.'

Further on is the room for pregnant women: comfortable armchairs, flowers, drawings on the walls. While they rest, they receive instruction in child care from the nurse.

A very small kitchen attracts our attention. 'That is for the workers of the Hwe minority,' Mrs Ting tells us.

'They eat separately?'

'Yes. Their religion forbids pork.'

We pay an impromptu visit to an elementary-school class. The night-shift workers are studying algebra with touching application.

We linger in the day-nursery, in the midst of attractive, happy, chubby babies, looked after by ravishing girls, more smiling and more human, we feel, than their sisters, the élite workers who run the machines.

We chat with the professors of the 'evening university' — young, enthusiastic, inspired by their work, convinced that they are intimately involved in the greatest revolution of history.

In the infirmary a curious incident throws a shadow over the picture. A young man whom we had taken for a Chinese sits up in bed when he hears us talk. 'Ah! you speak French! How marvellous!'

'You speak it very well yourself. How on earth — ?'

'That's easy to explain, I'm a Cambodian.'

'What are you doing here?'

'I was sent to study the technique of spinning cotton. I have been here a year, but I am to go home soon. It's the first time I've talked French for ages.'

The young Cambodian shakes our hands emotionally — there are tears in his eyes. Meanwhile our Chinese hosts are in a state.

'Do you speak Chinese?' we ask the young man.

'Alas, no. Only Cambodian and French. So you understand it's a pleasure to be suddenly talking French to some Canadians. Look, I have some French books.' And he waves a heavy geometry textbook at us.

'Are you very ill?'

'No — just some liver trouble. Oh! tell me a little about Canada.' The scene is really touching, and it seems to us that this conversation in French is doing the patient a world of good; he is beaming with pleasure.

Mrs Ting, the doctor, our interpreter, our guide, and our whole Chinese entourage are having an earnest discussion among themselves. Without understanding a word, we see that they feel they are in hot water. Yet our interpreter knows French, he would be able to translate after a fashion the very ordinary remarks we are exchanging with the Cambodian. But with a firm gesture Mrs Ting leads us out of the infirmary. 'You're tiring the patient,' she says. He himself seems only saddened to see us go.

Knowing the extreme tact and politeness of the Chinese, we have to conclude that it's a very serious business. Why? Could the Cambodian have given us revelations that they thought unsuitable? Probably not, but for safety's sake they would have felt bound to check the information beforehand. What was really serious was that the interview hadn't been 'foreseen' in the Plan. Oh, plan plan plan rata-plan . . .

After a good Chinese meal at the Peace Hotel — where the most utter peace reigns in the former English bars — we are taken to a rural commune, the Little Lake Commune, south of Shanghai.

The director is twenty-six years old. With only an elementary education, he is very much the commissar, and rather unappealing. However, he heads a commune of 23,373 inhabitants with a labour force of nearly 10,000, divided into 16 'brigades' and 138 'production teams'. The commune raises mixed crops — cereals, cotton, jute, and so on.

The director was to inflict a lecture of more than an hour on us. '*Before* the Liberation,' he says, 'the peasants were kept

down by the imperialists, the feudal lords, and the landed
proprietors. They lived in misery. *After* the Liberation, the
Communist Party and Chairman Mao gave them agrarian reform.
The results are sensational. From 1957 to 1960, production of
rice increased by 34.5 per cent, wheat 101 per cent, cotton 50
per cent, and pork 253 per cent.

'And the factories?'

'We have organized nine of them since the foundation of the
commune, principally to process and preserve our agricultural
produce.'

'Irrigation?'

'Eighty-three per cent of the whole area of the commune is
irrigated. The peasants' satisfaction is expressed in a poem that
is much in fashion just now.

> *'Technical irrigation is like a dragon:*
> *It can prevent drought*
> *And it can prevent floods.*
> *Now the great dragon plays*
> *An important part in our lives.'*

(Beware of Pi's prosody!)

'Is food supplied free as in some communes?'

'Rice is free, and this gives the peasants a great sense of
security. The commune has 148 restaurants, 145 day-nurseries,
and 43 kindergartens. The restaurants inspired this poem by
one of our peasants:

> *'The restaurant has greatly helped,*
> *The restaurant has emancipated, women*
> *To work for the community.*
> *Henceforth, women's work is never in their*
> *   own families.*
> *They have time for study and labour.'*

Things are going badly for Pi! But wait; the director continues:
'The increase in construction is equally important, and it inspired
this little poem:

'Formerly, we went to the fields to work
And we were shod in straw socks
And we came back barefoot from the fields.
Now, in fine weather, we are shod in cloth shoes,
And when it rains, we are shod in rubber shoes.
And when we go to town, we are shod in sport shoes.
And when we go to Shanghai, we are shod in
leather shoes.

'In spite of everything, there is a noticeable increase in bank deposits. In 1958 the peasants of this commune deposited 120,000 yuan [$48,000], in 1957 407,000 yuan [$162,800], in the first half of 1960 715,000 yuan [$286,000].'

'But what do the withdrawals amount to?'

'That is not known.'

'What is your school organization?'

'We have an agricultural high school, a general secondary school, and fifty-one elementary schools. In addition, we have our own telephone system and a small hospital.'

We visit the hospital, which is really just a clinic, established in the former residence of a great landowner. There are some seven doctors here, but the commune is said to have forty-two in all. For a rural population of 23,000, that seems rather a lot to us. After laborious explanations (Pi is mopping his brow), we understand at last that most of these doctors are not exactly that: they have 'high-school diplomas in medicine'. Some sort of nurses, we suppose.

There follows another discussion, quite as laborious, on the average wage paid by this commune (20 yuan per month, or $8) and that paid in Shanghai industry (65 yuan per month, or $26). 'We understand that the workers in the commune enjoy certain advantages, but all things considered they would still earn more in town. Why don't they go there?'

'Leaving nobody to produce food? That would be absurd.'

'No, no, the effect would be to establish some equilibrium between agricultural and industrial wages.'

'The Plan must adjust these inequalities in due course.'

'But meanwhile, isn't it unfair?'

'No. It is foreseen in the General Line, and the people are happy to work for the common good.'

'But a countryman isn't *free* to go and work wherever he wants?'

'He knows that the masses don't want him to go to the city.'

'Then he's *not* free?'

'Well! No, he's not free,' answers the director spiritedly. 'But your unemployed in capitalist countries, are they so free?'

That was horsefeathers, of course. But not such a bad answer for a Chinese peasant without much education; as a good Marxist, he knew how to find the chink in capitalism's armour.

On the road back we continue our discussion with the secretary of the Shanghai Cultural Association, a civilized and very intelligent man. In discussing theatre with him, Micheline Legendre had found that he was interested in what was happening elsewhere. In fact he is almost the only Chinese we have met who asks us questions. All the others, for all their lack of interest in Canada, claim to know better than we do what is going on there.

For once we have been able to put in a good word for our poor little Colombo Plan!

In the evening the Shanghai Cultural Association gives a banquet. There are dozens of dishes; but the hors d'oeuvres would be enough to satisfy our appetites.

To see the dedicated voraciousness with which our hosts gobble everything in their dishes, pouncing with their nimble chopsticks on the last grain of rice before it can escape the carnage, ransacking the fish-carcasses to find one more morsel of flesh, it is easy to believe that these are men who have known hunger.

Towards nine o'clock, having eaten and drunk too much, we have only one desire: to sleep. But no! Mr Hou waylays us and sweeps us into a room of the hotel where there will be two and a half hours of film 'for our foreign friends'.

It starts with an attractive cartoon in the style of Chinese watercolours: the amusing story of some newly hatched tadpoles looking for their mother among the dwellers in the river.

Next comes a long rigmarole in colour about 'the liberation of Woman in China' — wretched, unsubtle propaganda. Why show this to foreign visitors after a gargantuan banquet?

One thing, though: the lights are turned out. Nobody sees us glide towards the outer darkness, where there is no wailing or gnashing of teeth.

SATURDAY, 8 OCTOBER

The little party waiting for the boat on the Shanghai wharves is bathed in holiday sunlight. We would gladly go for a picnic on some Cythera covered with pagodas and marvels in jade. But more serious business awaits us: on the other side of the Hwang-Po is one of the old industrial districts of China, and there we are to meet a rare creature, a few specimens of which survive in captivity: a reformed capitalist.

The ferry crosses the river and deposits us in a sordid, dusty, crowded shantytown. Here is the Asia we used to know: the teeming promiscuity of the populous quarters of Saigon, Singapore, or Calcutta. The scandal is not that this degrading misery is still to be seen in China; the scandal is that in ten years the Communists have done more to diminish its empire than governments under capitalist domination had done in a hundred.

Decidedly Mr Hou has stopped taking us for imbeciles; he would have absolutely forbidden this trip if he had not believed us capable of making allowances. His impassive face betrays no anxiety, his mouth shapes no excuses.

But here we are in front of the China Woollen and Worsted Company, where we are to meet the reformed capitalist.

Everyone knows that the Communists summarily rushed to the gallows or to jail many of the great landed proprietors. It was the genius of Mao Tse-tung to realize the extent to which his revolution must depend on the peasants, and he mercilessly suppressed the class that inspired in these peasants awe, respect, and submissiveness towards outworn traditions.

In contrast the industrial revolution couldn't get off the ground quickly without the backing of the existing capitalist structure: the administrators, the technicians, the experts, and all the owner-managers who head great enterprises and make modern commerce function. At all costs the Chinese wanted to avoid the sovietization of the factories, that disastrous experiment that had nearly smashed the Russian Revolution and had forced Lenin to go into reverse with the NEP.

So Mao sought a *modus vivendi* that would allow him to incorporate into the new society all those whose experience and talent might be useful to the régime. A distinction was invented between the foreign capitalist and the national capitalist. The first was by definition an imperialist exploiter whom one could fleece and eject without scruple. The second could be transformed, thanks to that patient adaptability that characterizes the Chinese Revolution, into a 'reformed capitalist'.

We learned at the lecture on October the second what place was assigned to the reformed capitalist in the economic theory of industrial development. But here is a flesh-and-blood specimen awaiting us in the boardroom of China Woollen and Worsted.

Mr M. T. Lieu is a cultivated, pleasant, intelligent man. His correctness and his comportment still preserve a touch of England — where, as a rich man's son, he studied thirty-five years ago. He speaks English fluently, but affects the odd mannerism of screening his mouth with his hand as if to deflect the current of his speech. The interpreter intervenes less and less as communication establishes itself.

Mr Lieu is a survivor; also he possesses the faith of the miraculously healed. Or else he plays his hand marvellously well. First we hear the highly edifying tale of his conversion. He tells it with great facility, as if for the thousandth time . . .

In 1953 the factory became a mixed company: until his death in 1956, Mr Lieu's father shared its ownership with the State.

'Are you still co-owner of this factory?'

'Not now. I am the manager of the enterprise, and I get a salary of 500 yuan [$200] a month. In addition, since our family no longer owns my father's various enterprises, it receives five per cent a year on the invested capital of 20 million yuan. Out of that, I get 75,000 yuan [$30,000] a year.'

'Do you run the factory by yourself?'

'There's an assistant manager appointed by the State. Prices, wages, production, and expansion are determined by the Plan. If one enterprise is more efficient than another, its profits will be larger than foreseen, and part of these profits will be distributed among the workers. The balance will go to the State.'

'Are there still some capitalist enterprises today?'

'Not since 1956, except for some pedlars and very small shopkeepers. The State is the sole purchaser of products and the sole supplier of raw materials. As it favoured enterprises that had accepted co-ownership, the capitalists little by little came to understand that that would be an advantageous arrangement.'

'Will the situation go on evolving?'

'Yes. I think that before long they will abolish the five per cent paid to the former owners of capital. Certainly in 1962, at the end of the second Five Year Plan. Besides, money isn't everything — and I have enough to live on for the next hundred years! Even if, by 1962, all enterprises belonged wholly to the State, the former capitalists wouldn't complain. In eleven years they have had time to recognize the importance of the Communist reforms. For my part, I work much harder than before; sometimes my wife is amazed. But I like working, I feel my country belongs to me, and I am proud of taking part in its reconstruction. The government knows we are capitalists, accustomed to a certain standard of living. It takes account of that, and allows us still to have large incomes and a certain style of living. Besides, as there are no death duties, I shall be able to leave my estate to my family. Notice, too, that the State has already given my children all they need — education, leisure . . .'

A nice man, Mr Lieu, and perhaps we are wrong to receive some of his statements skeptically. And yet — from cross-checking later we find out that he is the same man who told the same story in the same tone to other travellers a few years earlier. From there it is just a short step to thinking of him as a 'show' reformed capitalist.

14 From the empty cathedral to the Children's Palace

It is the property of intelligence to perceive things in germination. — LAO TZU

Who should be waiting for us at breakfast but McIntosh in person, to whom we have said goodbye at least three times so far. He has incredible tales of tortoises to tell us. He studies tortoises, he collects tortoises, he already has five or six of them, which he is transporting from hotel to hotel, and he has just been offered another, an enormous one. These agreeable beasts live in his bathtub; but every time he leaves his room he has to hide them in damp cotton wool. Otherwise the hotel servants would relieve him of these unusual creatures.

We ask to go to mass, and are guided to the Cathedral of Zikawei. Six o'clock mass was the only one mentioned to us, undoubtedly so that we shouldn't 'lose' the morning, since there were so many *important* things to see in Shanghai. (We found out later that there were masses at seven, at eight, and even at five o'clock in the afternoon.)

Our hosts accompany us right to the door of the old Gothic church, but don't venture in. The great cathedral, where the strong Catholic community of Shanghai once thronged, is nearly empty; about a hundred of the faithful, mostly women, mostly old. There are no adolescents, except for five choirboys glimpsed in the sacristy. A Chinese priest of about fifty says low mass. The people take part devoutly; at least a third of them approach the altar. There is no sermon.

After mass we go to meet the priest in his sacristy. Our approach doesn't surprise him at all; he was forewarned. He speaks French fluently, but hastens to go and find his young curate, who 'speaks much better'. This is not exactly true, but it is to be understood that the priest has no desire to talk to us without a witness. Indeed, the curate is not enough. The organist, a layman, has to be found too. Advancement of the laity?

Tea is served in a drawing-room in the presbytery. A fine presbytery, with a lovely garden in full bloom. One would say that nothing had changed in ten years, if the coloured photograph of Mao Tse-tung hadn't replaced that of the Pope on the wall.

The parish priest, quite guileless by nature, seems pleased to be talking French to foreigners. But he doesn't chat much, leaving the initiative to the cold-eyed young curate, who greeted us unenthusiastically. He recites the catch-phrases of the reformers: 'The missionaries and the foreign bishops, even some brainwashed Chinese bishops, were spies who worked against our country on behalf of the imperialists, especially the Americans. For instance, during the Korean war, they told Chinese Catholics not to volunteer for the army on pain of excommunication. Imagine the moral conflict for Catholics.'

The objections we raise make him smile, and he goes on, harder than ever: 'Before, there was an enormous gulf between the clergy and the people. We lorded it over them. Not now. For example, at harvest-time we organize teams of priests who work for nothing. We even took part in the steel campaign, with our own small blast-furnaces. Like all true Chinese, we are patriots. Well, the foreign missionaries wanted to make spies of us. They forced us to learn French, to study even science and mathematics in French. Why?

'The missionary schools always taught more French than Chinese. Of course, shortly before the Liberation they hastened to appoint Chinese bishops. But how do you explain that only thirty were appointed in three centuries?'

That the missionaries made mistakes in China is admitted; and the battles of an enlightened missionary like Father Lebbe bear witness to it. But can this young curate really believe that they wanted to transform all the Chinese priests into spies?

We try to put some questions to the parish priest, who seems more serene than his young colleague. 'We were told that the Catholic seminaries were closed in China. Is that true?'

'Well, now . . . that's a hard question. The bishops were reactionaries, and since the seminaries were centres of opposition to the régime they had to disappear temporarily. We are re-organizing them — '

'Then they'll be functioning soon?'

'Yes, soon.'

That doesn't seem exactly certain.

How about relations with the Vatican? A cynical smile from the curate, but it is the parish priest who answers: 'There can be none so long as the Pope is linked with imperialism.'

'But if the Pope became, from your point of view, more liberal?'

'Impossible. He would cease to be Pope.'

Playing it their way, Hébert says: 'You don't believe in miracles?'

'Of course,' the parish priest answers, with a laugh. 'But the one you are imagining seems unlikely to me. The Church has always taken sides against progressive national governments. Hasn't that been demonstrated by its attitude to Cuba on the one hand, and Formosa on the other?'

'You would say that the Church is free in China?'

'Yes. Freedom of religion is guaranteed by the constitution.'

'Is it truly freedom when the State uses all modern means of propaganda to convert the people — especially the young — to Marxism, while the Church has no way of evangelizing but its pulpits, in churches that are empty or frequented by a handful of the already convinced?'

The parish priest splutters a little, and comes back to freedom of religion. 'We may teach religion to those who come and ask us to.' He keeps insisting on one point: religion is not dead.

'Can Catholic children belong to the Pioneers, the Communist youth movement?'

'Of course,' answers the priest. 'The Pioneers teach and develop high moral qualities, perfectly compatible with Catholic doctrine.'

'Does the Church still have its own youth movements?'

'No.'

'You admitted earlier that there was some incompatibility be-

tween Catholicism and Marxism; even so, can you denounce
Marxism from the pulpit?'

'We place as little stress as possible on the contradictions
between Marxism and Catholic doctrine.'

'Why?'

'Because we see clearly that the régime is good for the people.'

'What are the financial resources of the Chinese Church?'

'We used to own land. The State administers it and grants us
an income. The faithful give us some help, but collections have
never been a custom in our churches. Another cup of tea?'

The interview is apparently over. We take our leave of the
two priests, the naive one and the cynic, between them the more
or less conscious gravediggers of the Catholic Church in China.
Certainly there are priests who put up more resistance; they are
not shown to visitors, though.

When we get back to the hotel, we have a chat with our friend
Pi, that convinced and virtuous young Communist, about religion. 'Do you know any Chinese Catholics of your own age?'

'No.'

'Are there any?'

'Perhaps — I don't know.'

'If there are no young Catholics left, don't you think the
Church will eventually disappear from China?'

Pi is a nice boy; he doesn't want to hurt our feelings. He
smiles tactfully. 'It's hard to say. We'll see.'

But it is clear that for him religion is a memory of the past,
of vague superstitions that will soon be totally swept away by
the teaching of Marxist truth. 'If you like,' he says, 'we'll go
and see the Shanghai Children's Palace.'

That's his real answer to our question: the reader will shortly
see why.

The Children's Palace, once a French private club, is the chief
study and recreation centre of the huge youth movement called
the Pioneers.

The transition is violent, and it is easy to foresee which side
the future is on: after the half-dead cathedral, this palace filled

with sunlight and laughter, proud as a house of princes, humming with round-cheeked children, healthy, appealing, active.

About a hundred of them were awaiting us, commissioned to overwhelm us with their importunate friendliness. They are used to it, since every foreigner comes to see this place. That's not quite fair: Chinese children are charming even when nobody remembers to tell them to be. But it leaps to the eye that one boy and one girl have been told off to attach themselves to each one of us. With exquisite graciousness, the little couples take our hands and lead us from room to room. In one, children of twelve are learning classical ballet. In another, an admirable choir is singing a song in praise of Mao. 'And now,' the interpreter tells us, 'this is a song made up by a child!'

'Why are the children smiling? Is it a comic song?'

'It says "we must give the American imperialists a good punch in the nose".'

'Why teach hatred to children?'

'It's hatred for imperialists, not Americans.'

Are children of seven going to make the distinction?

On the teenagers' floor, we tour workshops where boys are building, with astonishing skill, boats and planes in lightweight wood, while girls are doing masterly embroidery — the most popular motif being the Picasso dove.

In the former ballroom, where blasé Europeans used to try to enjoy themselves, a few hundred children are doing folk dances, many of them straight from the 'fraternal countries' of central Europe. Our escorts drag us into the circle.

We think of the choirboys, glimpsed just now in the dim sacristy of the cathedral, putting on small cassocks, riddled with moth . . .

It's time for the regular cup of tea, which we are given in a sumptuously furnished room. The director would like to give us 'a few explanations'; but he spares us the customary lecture on the accursed imperialists and degenerate capitalists.

He explains the methods of the Pioneer Movement; they strongly resemble Baden-Powell's. The games, the sports, the singing, the dancing, the manual work, the rules, the Good Deeds, the patriotism, the citizenship, the sense of honour, the spirit of dedication and comradeship, the vaguely military salute, even to the scarf round the neck — the whole of scouting, except that the religion has been replaced by another, which lacks only God.

'What proportion of the children in Shanghai are Pioneers?' we ask the director.

'Ninety-five per cent. Their activities here round out the education they get from teachers and parents. We want to train élite workers.'

'What proportion of these children will become Communists?'

'A minority: forty per cent of young people belong to the Democratic Youth, and in the final analysis scarcely more than ten per cent of the citizens become members of the Communist Party.'

If one can judge by the Pioneers we have mingled with here and elsewhere in China, the attempt to infuse the youth of China with enthusiasm, indeed with fervour, has been successful. They throw themselves into their Pioneer activities with all the fire of their age. At twenty, they will be Marxists to the marrow.

One of the Canadians present, Denis Lazure, is a psychiatrist, and he asks permission to put a few questions to the children. 'What must you do to become a Pioneer?'

'Work well at school,' answers a boy of eleven.

'What is the worst fault a Pioneer can commit?'

'Pioneers never commit faults,' an urchin with sparkling eyes says gravely.

'What sort of good deeds must a Pioneer do every day?'

Several hands go up. 'If an old man is carrying a heavy load, help him,' says an adorable little girl with two apparently endless black braids.

'If two children are fighting, stop them,' says a boy.

'If you find something in the street, not to take it home but hand it over to the police.'

Exactly the Good Deed of the Cubs and Scouts . . .

Our psychiatrist asks about ten children, aged ten to thirteen, what they are going to be when they grow up.

The girls answer: 'A countrywoman because the country needs

good ones', 'a doctor', 'a scientist', 'an athlete', 'an actress', 'a worker', 'a dancer'.

The boys want to be scientists, mechanics, ordinary workers. The very slight and shy urchin holding Hébert's hand wants to be 'a brave soldier of the Red Army'.

In any event, what seems certain is that tomorrow these laughing children, gentle and charming, will be 'new men' in the Marxist sense. They were born at the same time as the régime, and it has nursed them along from the cradle, through the day-nursery, the nursery school, and the school; it organizes their recreation and guides them towards university with one well-defined aim: 'to change mankind'. And the régime knows that only at this price can it attain the ultimate goal: the creation of a Communist society.

The Chinese revolutionaries influence adults, they even give some attention to the old, but it is on the young that they found all their hopes. The old may sulk in their corner — what does it matter? The adults let themselves be carried along with the general enthusiasm, which is organized and irresistible. But it is these red-scarfed kids who in twenty years will be the New Men of a country which by that time will have a billion inhabitants.

And there are still good people who fiercely oppose the recognition of China, there are lunatics who dream of some incredible return by Chiang Kai-shek.

Every day we are asked if there is anything or anyone else we would like to see. This is stressed, but some of our requests get only half-answers.

For instance, Hébert would like to meet an ordinary Chinese journalist, in a private conversation, without an interpreter. Surely there are plenty of journalists in Shanghai who speak French or English. Hébert reminds Mr Hou of this every evening, and he always makes a note in his little book. But next morning our commissar never has a journalist to offer.

Today, however, Mr Hou announces that he has arranged the interview, but that Hébert must supply a list of the questions that he would like to put to the journalist. 'I should like to chat about rain . . . about fine weather . . . about whatever may come into our heads in the course of conversation.'

Mr Hou pouts. Hébert insists. But why the devil is it so difficult? Surely there must be one 'politically safe' journalist in Shanghai, one with the confidence of the régime, who could be allowed to talk to a 'capitalist bourgeois' journalist without a witness?

At three o'clock Mr Hou appears in Hébert's room, accompanied by one of the dignitaries who met us at the station the other day — 'the best-known journalist in Shanghai' in person! He has an interpreter with him. 'We really don't need an interpreter,' Hébert suggests.

'My English isn't good enough.'

'On the contrary, you speak it well.'

'All right, if you insist, we will speak English.'

'In that case you can let your interpreter go.'

'I should prefer him to stay.'

The interpreter didn't open his mouth once during the whole interview, but he was there, present, all ears. Is that why the conversation lacked warmth and the journalist contented himself with repeating party slogans?

We could ask almost anything of our Chinese hosts, and they actually refused us nothing — except to talk to a Chinese without a witness.

15 At Marxism School

Few people in the world hate with any understanding of the nature of what they hate. — CONFUCIUS

MONDAY, 10 OCTOBER

This morning we divide into two groups: Trudeau has an appointment with an economist, and Hébert is going to tour a teachers' college.

The principal of the Shanghai Teachers' College is a very subtle academic, who can muddle along in English and has a sense of humour. We make acquaintance around a huge tea-urn in the classic reception-room, adorned with photographs of great men: Marx, Lenin, Mao, and Stalin. While we have seen pictures of the first three everywhere, Stalin's is relatively rare in China. Still rarer is Khrushchev's.

In this gigantic college — it looks about as big as the University of Montreal — 750 professors teach 6000 students, and at the same time give correspondence courses for 5000 teachers and professors of the Shanghai region. According to the curriculum the college is divided into eleven sections: politics, pedagogy, the Chinese language, foreign languages (English and Russian), history, geography, geology, biology, mathematics, physics, and chemistry. The regular course is four years, not including three years of specialization.

'*Before,*' begins the principal, 'the quality of teaching in the teachers' colleges was very low. The only textbooks available to the students were in foreign languages (mostly English) or translated from them.

'*After* the Liberation, Chinese textbooks of excellent quality were brought out. In addition, we have a research centre, used not only by the professors but also by the more advanced students, which is an innovation in China. In accordance with the directives of the party, all our students do a great deal of manual work, in the rural communes of the region or in the factories. Half these students have working-class or peasant backgrounds, and a third of them are girls.'

'Have you problems of discipline?'

'Absolutely none — which was not the case before the Liberation. The students work eagerly and enthusiastically, because they recognize that the purpose of their studies is to contribute directly to the socialist enlightenment of our country.'

'Tuition is free, of course?'

'Not only tuition, but board, lodging, and medical care. We even give pocket-money to the less fortunate students. But there are no abuses, because everyone knows the State is poor.'

'Will your graduates teach in the Shanghai region?'

'It is the State that places all our graduates, according to the needs of the hour and each one's capacity. Even those who are destined for positions far from Shanghai accept this sacrifice joyfully. They know that before the Liberation teachers were badly paid and often unemployed.'

'How many hours of lectures a week do your students have?'

'Twenty-two, three of which are on Marxism-Leninism and three on international politics. In addition, their program includes ten hours of manual labour.'

'What is the average salary of your professors?'

'The first year, 49 yuan [$19.60] a month; the second year, 78 [$31.20]; the fifth year, 125 [$50]. Full professors attain 240 yuan [$96] a month.'

'How does one become a full professor?'

'The first criterion is the level of the professor's political consciousness. Secondly, we take account of his competence, and, finally, of his seniority.'

A long walk round the immense campus — full of flowers and divided in two by a little stream of brown water, which is entirely covered in many places with minute plants of a tender green. We remark to the principal that these water plants have a very pretty effect; he explains that they are grown to feed the pigs.

We visit classrooms, study halls, and a dozen laboratories furnished with modern equipment. There are some very complex electronic machines available for the use of the students. 'Are they made in China?'

'Yes,' says the principal with a smile, 'the Chinese manufacture machines as complex as these, and even export some. But for the sake of economy these ones are made by the students themselves.'

We have a feeling that the good principal is exaggerating. Evidently we fail to hide our incredulity, because we are led at once to a workshop where students aged eighteen to twenty, of both sexes, are in the very act of making similar appliances.

We spend an hour in the library — '870,000 volumes', says the principal offhandedly. As a test, Denis Lazure asks if they have any Western psychological journals. The librarian at once shows us recent issues of some thirty of them — German, English, French, American.

What strikes us most in the course of this lengthy tour is the intentness and solemnity of the students we meet in the lecture-rooms and laboratories, in the library, and on the campus. We can't help wondering if they ever take time for a little fun, if they relax on occasion. We have been told that foreign students are quite unhappy in China. Remember that these are always young Marxists from 'brother countries', élite students beyond question. They can't get used to the austerity of Chinese men, or the reserve of the women — even though this reserve is combined with exquisite graciousness. Caught redhanded in a harmless flirtation, the foreign student will be considered a degenerate, a bad Marxist; a stealthy pass at a fellow-student will put him in danger of being sent home.

While Hébert is strolling round the Teachers' College, Trudeau is meeting Panj Chi-yun, vice-president of the association of economists of Shanghai, accompanied by a younger economist, more inured to econometry.

Since Peking, Trudeau had been asked several times to specify in writing the questions he intended to put to the economists. He had agreed to confine himself to three problems: foreign investments in China, planning, and the future of capitalism.

On the first point, Mr Panj begins by emphasizing that, unlike capitalist countries, socialists cannot have recourse to war or to colonial exploitation to enrich themselves; they must rely mainly on accumulation and on savings.

'But there is certainly some foreign capital invested in China.'

'Before 1937, seventy per cent of our industrial capital was the property of the imperialists. Since the Liberation, there are no more imperialist investments; but we have been helped by the countries headed by the Soviet Union.'

'In fact, under the Sino-Soviet treaty of February 1950 the USSR lent you 1.2 billion roubles [$300 million or $120 million, according to which rate you use]. Are these credits exhausted, and have you begun to pay them back?'

'We don't know anything about that; it is a question for our government alone. But I can tell you that in October 1954 the Soviet Union granted us a long-term loan of 520 million roubles [$130 million or $52 million].'

'Are you free to spend this money wherever you like?'

'Certainly. China has itself made loans to other countries — Korea, Burma, Guinea. But some day we will have to reimburse the USSR, otherwise we would be in the position of exploiting its workers.'

'Would China be willing to borrow from capitalist countries?'

'If these countries could grant us conditions as advantageous as the USSR does (less than one per cent interest, for instance), we would see no objection to it. But in principle China must become increasingly self-sufficient; then it will no longer have any great need of foreign industrial capital. We don't like to be dependent on others. Soviet technicians are less and less needed in our country, and the same thing must become true of invested capital.'

The discussion then turns to the question of capitalism; it doesn't bring up anything interesting. Mr Panj methodically recites the main argument of *Das Kapital*. A state that is not the owner of its means of production cannot plan. Capitalism therefore cannot be self-correcting; it must be abolished. Until it is, profits increase and the misery of the masses becomes ever greater.

'But what you say doesn't correspond to the facts. In America, for instance, the standard of living never stops rising.'

'That is temporary, and can last only as long as the United States continues to exploit other countries. Besides, see how much unemployment there is in the capitalist countries; and they can only cure it by planning wars.'

'But what do you think of the theories of Keynes on economic stabilization?'

'We discuss Keynes a great deal; his theories don't resolve the contradictions inherent in capitalism.'

Passing next to the question of planning, Trudeau asks the economists if they know some of the Western economists who have studied socialist economics: Schumpeter and Lerner, for instance, or even the Polish economist Lange? They don't know them.

The discussion on planning is disappointing. They don't explain how prices are administered, nor how one estimates the demand for any given finished or partially finished product, nor how the economy attains equilibrium without being based on the law of supply and demand. They content themselves with reciting automatically the labour theory of value, and with repeating that the Plan decides everything.

Nor do they admit that errors of calculation may produce bottlenecks; and when Trudeau instances cases from his own observation they answer like the engineer at the automotive works: 'That is not an error; it is an indication of the zeal of the Chinese workers to exceed the Plan.'

The interview ends on this optimistic note. Decidedly, the mysteries of planning are not to be unveiled today.

In the three weeks since we arrived, we have still seen nothing of the Old China, except the Forbidden City (and the discoveries of our nocturnal explorations). We diffidently complain about this to Mr Hou and our Shanghai hosts. They seem as astounded as the executives of the Montreal Chamber of Commerce might be if foreign visitors were to demand to see the Indian reserve of Caughnawaga or the outside staircases of rue Saint-Denis.

Nevertheless the New China must have respect for its historic monuments, since it does restore them. (Unless it's a Department of Tourism getting ready for the future!)

Because we have insisted so much, we are taken to visit a Buddhist temple hidden away in an industrial quarter of the city. The monks have been forewarned, and they are awaiting us at the temple door. There are no young monks, as there always are elsewhere in the Orient; only middle-aged and old men, welcoming and smiling.

At the top of a very long staircase, we are asked to take our shoes off and put on thin rice-straw sandals: this is the Holy of Holies. An enormous jade Buddha fills a prayer-room with his peaceful presence. Seeing that we look more interested than the usual Soviet tourists, a monk leads us into a little room full of treasures: Ming statues, very old Buddhist manuscripts. He shows us ancient documents, surely priceless, and whispers incomprehensible explanations.

When we part from him, we salute the monk in the Buddhist manner, putting the hands together at chest level. He is pleased, and so are we, though Mr Hou and his suite seem anxious to get it over with. All the more since between three and six o'clock Trudeau is to have an 'important discussion on Marxism-Leninism'.

He has been demanding such an encounter since his arrival in China, and now he is introduced to Yung Chi, director of the Shanghai Institute of Social Sciences, and to Fong Chi, vice-president of the Society for Philosophical Research. These gentlemen define their functions as being principally concerned with research, and specifically research into the means of applying Marxism-Leninism to the Chinese situation. In consequence their knowledge of the social sciences, as they are taught in the West, is extremely limited. They have heard only vaguely, for instance, of the eminent English neo-Marxist, Harold Laski. This will make it all the more interesting to learn their opinions and prejudices about the West.

'What do you think of the future of the capitalist countries?' asks Trudeau.

'Capitalism has already entered its moribund phase, and it will die everywhere as it has died in China. Being founded on exploitation, such a régime plunges the masses into misery, until they decide to take their fate into their own hands.'

'But in many capitalist countries the masses enjoy a standard of living that keeps rising.'

'That is because the economies of these countries are based on the exploitation of others.'

'Cannot social democracy transform capitalism gradually? The Danes, for example, live well and exploit nobody.'

'There are progressive bourgeois, but they are incapable of resolving the fundamental contradictions of capitalism. The British Labour Party, for instance, is not truly socialist. Nevertheless it is for each nation to work out the solution it thinks just.'

'Then you believe in tolerance and peaceful co-existence?'

'We believe in it: no country has the right to use violence to overthrow another country's system of government. But we have to be ready for any eventuality; as Lenin said, as long as imperialism endures, the *possibility* of war will exist.'

There is nothing surprising in all this, and nothing to support the popular hypothesis of disagreement with the USSR. This is Marxist theory as it is universally accepted. So let's go on to questions of internal policy.

'Is China socialist or communist?'

'In Marxist-Leninist language, we are a socialist country; that is, we are still in the rudimentary phase of communism. The communes, for example, have elements of communism, but in so far as they are owned by the collectives and not by the State the material basis of communism doesn't exist.'

'Will the transition to communism take place soon?'

'It is impossible to say precisely. Such a transformation presupposes a more evolved social consciousness, higher educational and cultural standards, and greater material wealth. All that could take fifteen or twenty years.'

'Then you are evolving faster than the Soviet Union?'

'It is possible,' they answer with undisguised pride. 'But let us not forget that the USSR has given us a great deal of help.'

'What will happen to religion?'

'We believe it will disappear eventually, but that may take a long time. It is hard to say positively that there will be no more believers, even when the country has entered the communist phase. Anyway, believers will always have full political rights, and we shall respect their freedom and their customs.'

The discussion has been very cordial, but it must come to an end. It will at least have served, like the one with the economists this morning, to establish that the social sciences in China follow exactly the same line as Marxist textbooks the world over. In any case, if it was today that Trudeau was counting on receiving revelations and secret directives from the Chinese comrades (as he is reputed to have done from the Kremlin in 1952), he must feel terribly frustrated . . .

At seven in the evening the train leaves Shanghai. Three hours later we arrive at Hangchow, and discern extraordinary nocturnal silhouettes, sombrely reflected in a large lake. 'You'll see temples and pagodas here,' says Mr Hou with a smile. 'There's nothing else but!'

16 The peace of Hangchow

Why let yourself be astounded by the Ancients?

— CONFUCIUS

TUESDAY, 11 OCTOBER

Formerly a much-frequented place of pilgrimage, Hangchow is now first and foremost a holiday resort, a vast park whose sheet of ornamental water is the celebrated West Lake, surrounded by pagodas and pavilions, incomparable walks, and hotels. The most recent of these, built in 1956, is in the grand-hotel class — and that is where we are staying.

Mr Hou is relaxed and in an excellent temper; at Hangchow we are to have two days of bourgeois tourism. The timetable doesn't worry him. To miss a Shanghai factory is unpardonable; but if our unpunctuality forces us to omit a temple or two, Mr Hou makes gentle fun of it.

The day begins with a sampan ride on the West Lake. Mr Hou has unbuttoned his tunic; he lets his hand trail in the water and tells us about his children without having to be asked.

Like most of the Chinese we have met, Mr Hou is constantly amazed at the interest we show in his daily life, his family, and his recreations. You would think the Chinese were interested in nothing but Mao, the Great Leap Forward, Marxism, and the Red Army. After discussing all that so much, we are beginning to get depressed, and we should like to talk to our hosts about other things, to natter a little — to relax, for heaven's sake! But when we do it is always with a distinct sensation of lowering ourselves in their eyes.

At Hangchow, however . . .

In the middle of the lake is a flowering islet. We shall go and walk there, and get drunk on the powerful scent exhaled by the banks of lotus.

The beauties of this landscape have been sung by all the Chinese poets. It would be as ordinary as the most ordinary

Laurentian lake, however, if man had not added, over the centuries, all these charming structures, these trees, and these flowers.

'*Before* the Liberation,' our local guide tells us, 'the reactionaries had *destroyed most of the beautiful landscapes.*' Good, the official jargon is beginning; let us close our inner ears. All officials have been to the same school, that is clear from their language. And bitter experience has taught us to pay no more attention to their stereotyped formulae than if they were so many belches.

At first, when the Chinese said, 'We have our weaknesses . . .', we had consented to point out a few of them. But we understood at last that that made them look on us as rank liars. In the museum, when the guide had said, 'Before the Liberation the people in their ignorance used to melt down ancient objects of art; since the Liberation, we preserve in the museum everything that the foreign imperialists didn't carry off,' we had answered that thanks to the Metropolitan and the British Museum some Chinese antiquities had at least been saved from the melting-pot; and that if all the museums of the world had to return their works of art to their countries of origin, Leningrad would lose a good many Egyptian mummies, Greek sarcophagi, Polynesian masks, and French Impressionists. But we were given to understand that these quibbles were the height of rudeness.

After that we stopped wincing. When a sentence began with 'The Kuomintang reactionaries supported by the American imperialists . . .', we knew we were going to have to let the explanation of some misfortune pass — for example, the fact that there were still some mental patients in this country. When a speech began, 'Before the Liberation . . .', we could stop listening until the end of the second half of the sentence, 'After the Liberation . . .'. The formulae had begun to leave us cold: 'The Chinese Communist Party led by Chairman Mao . . . the Soviet countries under the leadership of the USSR . . . to build socialism rapidly, well, and efficiently . . .'. You can have them: the General Line, the leadership of the masses, the Great Leap Forward, and all.

In general we were as deaf to this jargon as to their stutters, or to the perpetual '*jiga, jiga*' with which the Chinese sprinkle their conversation. (The Chinese '*jiga*' is the equivalent of our hesitant 'uh'. Trudeau had assimilated it so well that in his formal speeches in French or English he kept disconcerting his translators by putting '*jigas*' in the most unexpected places.)

Coming back to these beautiful landscapes that the reactionaries had destroyed: the islet, the parks, and the walks along the shore of the lake are full of tourists with cameras and peanuts — Chinese tourists, 'workers on holiday', Mr Hou insists, students, and convalescents. These people are so sober and correct even on holiday that one sometimes wonders whether they are enjoying themselves.

In one corner of the lake, three small stone towers rise out of the water. Each of them has five holes pierced in it, and during the mid-August festival candles are placed inside; fifteen moons are then reflected in the water, not counting the real one.

We linger by a pond filled with thousands of goldfish. If you merely throw in some breadcrumbs the water instantly seethes and reddens as if a shark had just been disembowelled.

They stuff us with pagodas: the Pao Chou Pagoda, set on the Hill of the Precious Stone, tapered like a Gothic spire; the Pagoda of the Six Harmonies, built a thousand years ago. We visit the Lin Yin Temple, its thousand-year-old grottoes adorned with sculptures inside as well as outside. An itinerant photographer, of the sort that is found on the fringes of all the historical monuments of the great tourist centres of the West, is taking pictures of happy couples in front of a gigantic Buddha. Private enterprise?

Close to a temple there flows a spring of clear, cold water from which, it seems, the best tea in China is made. We sample several cups of it with a beaming Mr Hou, who explains to us why this spring bears the name of Tiger Spring. Centuries and centuries ago there were two tigers, which burrowed and burrowed until — but a terrible roar interrupts our commissar. There are still tigers, very close by, in a cage. We go to see what they think of Mr Hou's explanations. But it is a lion that chiefly fascinates us: as a companion he has a puppy, with which he plays unwearyingly. The dog snaps bravely at his muzzle, the lion retorts with a mighty blow of his paw.

All good fun, it's the holidays.

But Mr Hou . . .

He proposes that we should visit a sanatorium in the afternoon and, of course, a factory tomorrow. And in the evening two very long war films, although we had been promised only one.

The first, in black and white, is an episode of the Korean War, in the customary style of war films: the gallantry, patriotism, and courage of a company that finally captures the coveted position. The American soldiers are caricatured, but less spitefully than the Americans caricature the Chinese in their films on the same subject. It lasts two hours, and all the time Pi is trying desperately, through the din of bombs and machine guns, to translate the dialogue for us.

Then, the main feature: a huge contraption in colour recounting the capture of Shanghai by the Red Army. With edifying zeal, Pi talks himself breathless. Quite uselessly, moreover; it is easy to guess at the noble speeches of the alert, energetic young Communist officers, and the base sentiments of the gross Kuomintang officers as they soak themselves in Rémy Martin. In exasperation we take French leave under cover of a bombardment, intending not to come back till the end of the film. We walk through the ill-lit streets without meeting anyone; there is no reason to stay up later at Hangchow than in Shanghai.

We come back at midnight, confident that the film is over by this time. Not at all, the battle is still raging. But the few foreigners in the hotel have surrendered their arms and burned their colours. Still standing up and taking it are Mr Hou, Pi, and the hotel staff — even though they have to get up early in the morning. They seem to be enjoying it, and it is not the first time these two patriotic turkeys have been shown in this hotel.

Swarms of theatrical companies and film-projection teams traverse China in all directions to carry 'people's art' into the most remote villages; a 'scarcely artistic art', as Savignac would say, centred on the themes of official propaganda. The State cannot take the risk of dispensing with this vast effort at persuasion. The enemies of the New China assert that it is by machine guns and bayonets that the Chinese are made to work so hard. In fact a better way has been found: plays and films, which lead the masses to *think* along the régime's lines, and to accept the effort demanded of them.

Obviously there are all the other methods of persuasion; the régime neglects none of them. A Chinese is besieged: in the factory he is served up party slogans by means of posters, banners, and loudspeakers; he will read the same slogans in the newspaper, hear them a hundred, a thousand times on radio and television, and then find them in another form in exhibitions of painting, and even in the temples and churches if he still goes to them.

But the most effective (and least costly) method of persuasion is perhaps the district meeting. Here the whole family is indoctrinated. Fanatics carry the hesitant along with them, father convinces son, son persuades father, wives who have 'won their freedom' give the coup de grâce. Lastly, well-trained propagandists go from one meeting to another to stimulate the local leaders.

Is it obligatory to go to the district meeting? Neither more nor less obligatory than it is for our own Catholics to go to mass. Some go to the meeting with the enthusiasm and zeal of true believers. Others go to it, as some go to mass, to avoid committing a social error. As a result almost all Chinese attend the weekly indoctrination meetings. What religion has been preached so effectively, and by so many means?

There is much talk in our newspapers of a reign of terror in China. This is a poor explanation of the matter. Why antagonize a whole region by massacring discontented peasants when it is so simple to send an army of propagandists who will transform recalcitrants into convinced Marxists, into zealous and possibly into cheerful workers? Certainly the Revolution was not established without violence, but why would the revolutionaries continue to resort to it when they have found, in persuasion, a better way?

'But after all,' the doubter will say, 'surely the Chinese don't accept such a régime cheerfully; they are intelligent. Aren't they bound to resist all that propaganda?'

The ancient enemy of China is hunger. It had been in occupation of the whole country for millennia; ten years ago it was still defying the people. Crouched before every door like a menacing dragon, it killed Chinese by tens of millions. Who was it that vanquished this implacable enemy? Mao.

That fact alone would be enough to explain the behaviour of this ancient civilization, which one would have expected either to vomit up Marxism or to assimilate it, as it has assimilated everything that has come from the foreigner. Mao conquered hunger, and told the Chinese that it was thanks to Marxism. Hence the Chinese put their trust in the régime.

It is not a matter of promises: control of the waters by dykes and dams, afforestation, reclamation of land, mechanization of agriculture, expansion of industry, and above all the bowl of rice or the loaf of bread on every table in China — these are facts that each Chinese can verify at the ends of his chopsticks.

'Hold on a minute, please! Isn't famine raging in China at this very moment?'

Do you mean the famine in which the conservative press of the West takes such delight? The famine of which the Formosan government speaks with such cheerful compassion? It is true that dispatches from Hong Kong report a 'shortage of provisions that in some districts verges on famine'. It is true that during our journey people mentioned to us droughts in the south and floods in the north. That while there was 'no rationing' there was 'controlled distribution' of foodstuffs. All the same, it has to be acknowledged: it would take more than that to overturn the government of Mao Tse-tung.

It has been related in the West how the Russian famine of 1932 killed millions of people. Well, the outcome of that was an increase in Stalin's dictatorial power. However, famine was not as common in Russia as in China, where it has been known for thousands of years. That takes nothing away from the tragedy of today's outbreaks. But as long as they are less frequent and less deadly than those of yesterday, the Chinese will be conscious of progress and hopeful that it will continue.

In fact a famine of the same gravity today will do less harm than in the past, for there will be no financial sharks to speculate in misery. And the instruments of distribution and apportionment (roads, trucks, staff) are better organized today than they used to be.

Conclusion: the Chinese will continue to listen to the teachers of Marxism at the weekly meeting.

'But still, it's a totalitarian régime — a dictatorship!'

Of course. Chiang Kai-shek and the emperors were also dictators, but their power was not directly founded on the people, and they were not so well organized for giving thought to the people's problems. The present régime, in contrast, since it attacks the feudal lords, the capitalists, and the superstructures of the old days, is bound to be as little alienated as possible from the Chinese masses. And it takes the trouble to convince them of its good faith, to convert them to its teaching. *By every means.*

WEDNESDAY, 12 OCTOBER

Tourism in the morning. A bamboo forest, the Grotto of the Yellow Dragon (the dragon is carved from the living rock, and a real spring courses from his mouth), parks, temples, the Sun Yat-sen garden. In one of the temples a Buddhist monk in need of a shave gives us a short propaganda talk, which we have been spared hitherto in Hangchow. 'You see our magnificent Buddha?'

Yes, he is beautiful. To be precise, he is too beautiful: pomaded, clean, freshly lacquered.

'After the Liberation we had no Buddha, as the old one had been destroyed. Then the government offered to pay for a new one for us, and we organized a competition among the artists. A discussion arose over the final choice. Well, it was Prime Minister Chou En-lai himself who settled the question, thus showing how much interest he takes in Buddhism.'

Better not count on it!

'Hangchow is the silk capital,' Mr Hou tells us, by way of explaining that you couldn't stay forty-eight hours there without touring a spinning-mill.

It's a very Hangchow factory, looking like a park in which every pavilion is a workshop. There are flowers everywhere. There is a flowerbed of green plants with ideograms formed of red plants — the now familiar ideograms signifying 'Long live the General Line!'

Admirable brocades are made here, on old wooden looms. We linger in the workshop where those famous natural-silk tapestries are woven. 'Before the Liberation,' the directress of the factory tells us, 'only traditional subjects were treated, often inspired by famous paintings: flowers, birds, butterflies. Since the Liberation we have made pictures of real life.'

What a pity that all these skilful hands, all these genuine artists should now be reduced to the production of a series of chromos of surpassing ugliness, of landscapes that are exact copies of photographs and postcards. A specialty of the house: photographs of Mao, Chou, and other big wheels, faithfully reproduced on semi-automatic looms. They don't even conceal the large wart Mao has on his chin. It seems it's a symbol of good luck!

We walk along the shore of the lake, where athletes are training for canoe races. In black bathing suits, girls (of a sort we hadn't thought existed in China) impress us. By their athletic performances, of course. Children surround us and, shrieking with laughter, allow us to take their pictures.

When we get back to the hotel, who should be awaiting us in the lobby but McIntosh, alone as always, and delighted to rediscover the ersatz Britishers that we are. We exchange impressions, compare experiences. Then, farewell once more, since our timetables and itineraries don't coincide.

A farewell banquet, princely as ever. Two Hangchow specialities worth recommending: fish from the West Lake in sweet sauce, and shrimps fried in green tea-leaves.

The toasts are numerous, but not, fortunately, the speeches. For we are catching the train for Canton at nine this evening.

17 Canton

It is the teachers who have caused the disorder in the world.

— CHUANG TZU

A long day on the train, with nothing worth reporting except increasing warmth. After the rather gloomy autumn of the north-east, it is good to taste the delightful climate of south China.

We take advantage of the journey to reflect on the economic plan. The train is on its way; we have to listen to each other. The reader is better off: he can leave the train, and the paragraphs that follow, and pick us up again tomorrow. So we'll see you at Canton station at six o'clock in the morning.

We recall that at the end of each meeting there was one question we always asked, in one form or another: 'In a planned economy, and when prices and production are not regulated by supply and demand, who makes the decision — and how? How does the carpet factory or automotive works know how much to produce and when to expand? How does the commune divide its yield between its own members and the State? Who decides the scale of wages and the rate of profit?' And always we got the same answer: the Plan. The Plan was the source of every attitude, the fountainhead of all decisions, the bosom in which every anxious manager could find security.

Well *(jiga, jiga)*, in a country where entrepreneurial talent is exceedingly scarce, such a system has its points. When the local manager doesn't have to worry about his raw materials or his markets, when his payroll and his rate of investment are decided by others, he can devote his efforts to increasing production. That is to say, he will concentrate all his energies on fulfilling or exceeding the Plan. And that is why, on the one hand, competition within each factory will be encouraged by all kinds of banners, rolls of honour, and improvised fanfares; and on the other, the workers will be encouraged to invent all kinds of gimmicks to improve output. The result can only be increased production — in certain sectors of industry or certain areas of the national economy. But in practice this also means bottlenecks.

And in fact do you remember those fields strewn with engines, those endless streets cluttered with railway coaches and tubing, in Shenyang? Those were glaring examples of bottlenecks in the execution of the Plan. Yet the economists and engineers we questioned refused to see them as anything but glorious indications of continuously increasing productivity. Their attitude endorsed a combination of economic waste and technical efficiency that would make any Western economist or entrepreneur shudder.

But the Chinese gloried in it! And perhaps they weren't altogether wrong. After all, the Chinese industrial revolution was just born, and already it was growing at a staggering rate. Perhaps that couldn't have been done without imbuing managers and workers with a single obsession — to surpass the Plan.

The workers work, the managers manage, and the problems that result from bottlenecks and dislocations land in the laps of regional and national planners. On them devolves the task of readjusting the plan from year to year and from month to month. Certainly it's not easy, under a system where rather blunt administrative tools have to take the place of precise economic indicators. But they must console themselves by quoting Chairman Mao: 'In our country an economic plan is drawn up every year to establish a suitable ratio between accumulation and consumption, and to attain equilibrium between production and the needs of society. . . . This equilibrium and this unity are partly broken every month, every quarter, requiring a partial readjustment. Sometimes, when the arrangements made fail to correspond to reality, contradictions occur and the equilibrium is disrupted. That is called committing an error. Contradictions appear unceasingly, and are unceasingly resolved. That is what constitutes the dialectical law of development of affairs and of phenomena.'

Well, what can you say? That planning in China today consists in part of one simple slogan: 'More'. And that in part it is a process of continual readjustment in the light of production standards that keep changing as the new working class goes through its apprenticeship.

Obviously such a rudimentary economic process is bound to give rise to gigantic errors — gluts and bottlenecks. But they will be corrected in the next revision of the Plan; and, as for the embarrassing surpluses, an effort will be made to direct them into the vast markets of Asia and Africa. Indeed, in China itself takers can be found for almost anything — even if it does require the use of capitalist-style advertising posters!

This, we conclude, is not the tidy planning taught in the great faculties of economics. But is it not the awkward, befuddled awakening of a formidable industrial giant?

No answer. For sleep has long since invaded the railway car as it rolls peacefully along beside the legendary River of Pearls.

FRIDAY, 14 OCTOBER

Six o'clock in the morning. A reception committee is waiting for us.

Canton was one of the most active revolutionary centres, and it was here that Mao trained the peasant leaders, without whom the revolution might never have taken place. Our hosts plunge us into the right atmosphere at once by taking us to see the famous school where Mao used to teach. Founded in 1924, it was an official school in the beginning; at that period relations between the Kuomintang and the Communist Party had not yet been broken off.

We meet the director, and drink tea amidst a dreamlike décor: a sort of patio, full of tropical plants and heavy furniture of carved wood.

We are accompanied by a pretty young Chinese, her too-solemn face framed in thick black braids, no doubt a secretary in the local Cultural Association. She is very graceful in her simple cotton print, white with big green polka-dots; the skirt reaches below her knees, in the style of 1947. Is she twenty? Anyway she is too serious for her age: our most improbable jests draw from her no more smiles than are called for in 'the general plan'.

Together we tour the school, which is now a museum, a shrine, a place of pilgrimage. 'That is the bedroom occupied by the principal of the Revolutionary School,' says the director with emotion. A minute's silence. 'This was the teachers' common-room.' Mr Hou raises his cap. 'And the dining-hall . . .' Tables and benches of rough wood. And finally: 'There is Mao's modest bedroom.' Emotion is at its height. We gaze silently on the camp-bed, the desk, the chair . . .

Back to the Hotel Aichun ('Love the Masses'), which is rather dismal and desperately empty. But the view makes up for every-thing; from our ninth-storey window the River of Pearls is a pure marvel; from here, one would never suspect its foul stench.

The scene has an unreal quality, especially at night. The junks look like great butterflies, their black wings folded on their long brown bodies; the sampans suggest fireflies, carrying their little lamps along with the current. They glide by in their hundreds, noiselessly and irresistibly, like spruce logs on our rivers. These boats are so loaded down with rice, or rusty metal, or human manure, so encumbered with passengers and crew, that if the helmsman made one false move they would be swallowed up in the muddy waters.

Whole families live on these sampans, four feet wide and fifteen feet long. The babies are attached to ropes that give them enough play but allow them to be fished out whenever they fall in the river. As soon as they have the strength, they will learn to work the steering-oar. Here is one kind of Chinese that is still remote from the day-nursery and the communal restau-rant. Are they to be envied?

In Canton — with its three million inhabitants the largest city of the south — we rediscover something of the poverty-stricken China of yesterday, where men had learned to die of hunger without complaint, or to live on nothing — a pair of trousers, a shirt, a mat to unroll on the family sampan at night, a bowl of rice, a morsel of fish. Mr Hou has told us nothing about it, but it is clear that at least on the River of Pearls there are still

Chinese who work more than eight hours a day; at least in Canton there are still coolies, pushing or pulling enormous loads, bodies running with sweat, faces haggard.

We spend part of the evening in the Park of Culture, which was set up as far back as 1951. Exhibitions of art, of flowers, and of Chinese lanterns; theatres, open-air concerts, films, marionettes. A room for chess-players, a basketball field floodlit at night, a skating-rink, ping-pong, badminton; all this scattered through a park full of trees and flowers.

The huge crowd mills about noiselessly, as if it were walking on tiptoe, stopping for an hour at the open-air theatre before going on to admire the acrobats or listen to the symphony orchestra. They hold the children up above their heads to give them a good view of the musicians.

Our hosts are determined to show us an exhibition of the works of the students of the Canton School of Fine Arts — which, it must be said, attracts a smaller crowd than the acrobats. Our guide draws to our attention — though it actually hits you smack in the eye! — that the young artists of China have abandoned 'flowers and butterflies' for tractors, blast-furnaces, muscular workers, and peasant women planting red flags in the rice-paddies.

But then how can you explain the popularity of old Chi Pai-shih, the modern painter who just died at nearly a hundred years old? This great artist — born, it is true, in the same village as Mao — painted only flies, grasshoppers, flowers, fruits, and, above all, crabs and rats, with the traditional simplicity and economy of Chinese art, but also with the freshness and clarity of modern art. As far as we know, Chi Pai-shih never conformed to Moscow-inspired socialist realism. And he stayed in favour with the régime until his death.

On leaving the park Hébert and Trudeau, deciding to go for a walk in Canton, take leave of the group. Mr Hou points out that tomorrow's program is very full and we'll have to get up early. We insist. Our Cantonese hosts look disconcerted, but Mr Hou is accustomed by now to our escapades (which are relatively rare, after all), and just gives us an imploring look. All it takes is a little firmness: shake hands with everybody and off we go. Before our hosts recover from their surprise we are far away, lost in the crowd under the ill-lit arcades.

It's ten-thirty. We are in a hot country, and no doubt that's why people stay up later than in the north. Also, the people are more talkative and relaxed. Scandalous! — there are cafés where young couples are quietly sipping orangeade. In a confectionery, girls wrapping up toffee explode with laughter under their surgical masks. We peer into a day-nursery and see babies in very clean beds, dreaming of angels — well, at least they're too young to be dreaming about Mao.

For the first time in China we see women and children pursuing the wretched little trades of the streets: urchins of ten or twelve are shining shoes, women sitting on the sidewalks are offering a few fruits for sale, or a dozen red peppers laid out on a handkerchief. At least there is no soliciting, and there are no longer any beggars, as there used to be; evidently the professionals have been mercilessly compelled to work . . .

Western travellers who visited Canton four or five years ago still spoke of small prostitutes whose mothers offered them to passers-by, or who offered themselves with little animal-like cries. That is now a memory of the past. The former prostitutes are being re-educated into shock-troops of labour and 'excellent Marxists'.

It is as mild as a July night. We don't get tired of walking, sniffing at the shops and stalls, watching people as they argue and buy and eat ice cream and read the newspaper. This is a hot city, where clothing is sketchy and at night you see people asleep on the pavement in front of the open doors of their shops.

Why did Mr Hou want to deny us this pleasure? Was it to keep us from witnessing the excrement-collection that takes place at this hour? (Hence the name 'night-soil'.) We are quite bright enough to realize that the régime couldn't in eleven years bestow a complete sewage system on a country of 650 million people which had done without one from the beginning of time.

In fact in the little streets in the heart of Canton we can't help meeting the excrement collectors and their travelling cesspits. Carrying wooden buckets, they go into every house and work in silence as if they were performing a shameful act. Yet it is thanks to this manure, eventually dumped in the gardens, that the cabbages and lettuces of China are so fine.

But that is another example of the vicious circles that have always kept the Chinese in misery. The soil was poor, so the townsman had to send something to fertilize it. But he was sending at the same time the causes of typhoid and other diseases. In defence, the food, and the water to be used for tea, had to be carefully sterilized. Fires perpetually alight for this purpose used up as fuel the wood and other vegetable matter that would otherwise have fertilized the soil with their humus. So the manure had to come from man, and this brought epidemics *unless* the humus was burned up . . . So the devilish cycle grew worse from century to century. There are some things, it seems, that cannot be changed short of a revolution.

Our walk had taken us as far as the river. Trudeau wanted to revisit the Isle of Sha-mun, the erstwhile strictly exclusive retreat of the consular corps and of wealthy foreigners — Chinese came to it only as domestics. The traveller of '49 described a peaceful 'green' at the centre of the island, and magnificent houses around the edge. He also summoned up the recollection of certain dives where it had not been hard to console oneself with what Chiang had made dangerous — visits to opium dens.

Tonight everything is different. The houses and apartments are populated by Chinese exclusively. Through wide-open windows we see humble interiors, with clotheslines and rows of pallets. Along the boardwalk are Chinese lovers holding hands, and squatting men playing chess. And moored to the shore are evil-smelling sampans.

SATURDAY, 15 OCTOBER

Mr Hou is fidgeting from seven-thirty on. He comes and shakes us in our beds, saying things that Pi doesn't bother to translate, their tenor is so obvious: 'Up you get! You've got to hurry! There's a big rural commune to tour! Quick!'

The Commune of the Flowery Mountain is situated an hour and a half from Canton in the direction of Changsha, at the end of a dusty road that is still under construction. It is being built without machinery; hundreds of men and women are carrying earth and stones, each one with two small straw panniers hanging from a yoke.

Mr Tung, the director of the commune, is a very young man, bursting with enthusiasm and pride in the fantastic figures with which he is about to stun us. Nibbling dry lichees and drinking our tea, we listen to his speech. 'Our commune was organized in 1958 out of eighty-eight advanced agricultural co-operatives. It comprises 13,830 families, forming a population of 60,020 who are divided into 286 production teams and sixty-two brigades. The chief crop is rice, but we also cultivate sweet potatoes, sugar cane, tobacco, peanuts, and lichees. And we raise pigs, chickens, ducks, and geese.'

Taking us, no doubt, for a delegation of agronomists, Mr Tung spares us no detail. '*Before,* this population used to suffer from hunger caused by the exploitation of the great landed proprietors. The rice-paddies were short of water, and we had to buy our rice in the neighbouring countries. In 1949 our peasants were living on porridge and wild vegetables. The four great scourges of China rarely passed us by — flood, drought, wind, and insects used to arrive regularly at harvest-time. The peasants were forced to flee the district, and often to exile themselves; thousands left us at that time to settle in Singapore, Vietnam, Indonesia, Panama — and even Canada.'

We knew, in fact, that most Chinese-Canadians were originally from the Canton region. But there was another sign that we were in a zone of emigration: every now and then we had been surprised to come across a sort of fortified manor-house, several storeys high though it was built in an open field. We learn now that these curious structures, totally un-Chinese in style, were built by Chinese who had come back to China to end their days after making their fortunes overseas. There were three advantages to this kind of dwelling: they expressed opulence, they were proof against the banditry that used to be common, and they were spacious enough to allow the patriarch to bring his numerous descendants together under his roof in order to put them to work in his fields.

'*After* the Liberation,' Mr Tung continues, 'everything changed. In 1954, 1955, and 1956, there were food shortages caused by the four scourges, and the government had to supply us with rice. In 1958 we were able to produce enough for the needs of the immediate neighbourhood. In 1959 we built several reservoirs and important works of irrigation, with the result that the harvest that year surpassed anything we could have imagined. We managed to buy nineteen tractors and eight trucks for the commune and to set up twenty workshops. In one of these workshops, equipped with twelve lathes, we make agricultural machinery for our own requirements.'

Next, education 'before' and 'after': '*Before*, the children were starving, and they couldn't go to school. *After* the Liberation the situation changed completely. Now we have 16,200 children in the schools of the commune. This autumn we are sending twenty-eight students to the Universities of Peking, Nanking, and Canton. There are three libraries in the commune. Finally we have 11,000 children in day-nurseries and kindergartens, so that a woman can go to work in the fields without having to carry her youngest on her back.'

We are given a lunch whose very simplicity makes it pleasanter than the customary banquet, and afterwards we go to inspect an irrigation canal about two miles long, which carries water from a nearby river to the commune. It was built in two months, but it must have put the commune about ten years ahead. Even before the water irrigates the fields it works a mill for husking the rice. Soon it will supply electricity to that part of the commune.

Next we go up to the high ground of the commune to visit an immense reservoir, built in a hundred and five days by thousands of arms carrying panniers of soil, with the help of only two tractors. It is a real lake, fifty feet deep. As well as providing reliable irrigation, it contributes to an improved diet, having been stocked with six hundred thousand fish.

On top of the dam is a pavilion in the Chinese style, and here we rest. The director of the commune has brought two watermelons, which we share like brothers.

We reflect on the impression that must have been made on

the Chinese peasant by these immense works of irrigation that have transformed the valley spread out at our feet, and by those patient reforestation projects that are re-clothing the mountains where we are perched. It's not hard to believe that these people are filled with hope as they labour, when they see their own efforts are putting an end to three thousand years of erosion, drought, and floods.

That is what Westerners fail to see behind all the absurdities related by their newspapers for the last two years. *Even if* the communal system had turned all China into a mass of labour camps (and it is hard to believe that the Chinese would have preferred to stay in their former servitude and misery) — *even if* the commune has to turn over a large share of its proceeds to the State (and it can't be more than the tributes formerly exacted by the feudal landlords) — the communard *sees* the soil producing more than it used to, and he *knows* that the share levied by the State goes to enrich China, not Japan, England, or France.

Certainly there must have been, must still be excesses. Perhaps the readers of *Life* were not being hoodwinked when they were asked to commiserate with parents separated from their families, or married couples waiting in line on Saturday night for their turn at a few minutes in a borrowed bed.

Every revolution produces its fanatics, and no doubt some regions have suffered from an excess of zeal. But the zealots are not in power, and they have even been denounced by Mao's government — that, in fact, is how the Hong Kong correspondents have been able to establish the existence of abuses.

Our own experience is that in all the communes we have seen the single-family dwelling is the rule, which suggests that that is what the régime officially prefers. It is true that 'the Chinese family has been broken up', but that is the *patriarchal* family, praised by Confucius and imposed by a thousand-year-old decree that required four generations of the same family to live together. So what shocks Westerners is that China is reaching today the stage of the *conjugal* family (i.e., father, mother, and children, but no great-great-uncles), which began to establish itself in the West at the start of modern times. When that is said, and calmly accepted, the commune appears quite simply as what it is: a much-needed administrative reform, and a step towards socialism.

Consider it first as an administrative reform. Pre-Communist China was excessively bureaucratic. The commune does away with the obsolete structures of counties and municipalities, and replaces them with economically functional units. In this way the commune will group together several units (say, a highland community and a market-gardening one) that used to be distinct and whose economies are complementary. At the same time they avoid systematically grouping a poor unit with a rich one; the tendency is rather to require the former to compete with the latter.

The commune is also a step towards socialism, in that it broadens the base of collective ownership beyond what was established in 1951 with the step of mutual aid, in 1954 with the co-operatives, and in 1956 with the higher co-operatives. But the commune is not yet communism — the principle is 'to each according to his work', not 'according to his need'. We observed this just now, watching the women coming in from the fields and getting credit equivalent to the amount of the crop they were carrying on their yokes.

Such were our meditations as we sucked on our watermelons in a little pavilion suspended between the lake and the setting sun. But a few points remained to be cleared up. 'If a worker were to choose to spend his time on his own ducks and his own little plot of ground, would his profit be greater, perhaps, than if he had gone to the communal fields?'

'There is no longer any egoism in the commune.'

'If a young man from the commune has finished his higher education, is he free to choose between town and country when he starts his working life?'

'He will naturally return to work where he came from: that is to say, in the country.'

'But what if he prefers the city?'

'His placement is determined by two factors: his own choice, and the "will of the masses".'

'But supposing they conflict?'

After a lot of questions, the director of the commune finally acknowledges that at present, according to the Plan, all the workers are needed on the land. Besides, a city employer who is conforming to the Plan would have no way of paying a new employee who came to offer his services — unless his marginal productivity was extremely high.

We conclude that peasants' sons are at liberty — to stay in the rural commune; and that this will be so until the Plan decrees an urbanizing process. Then, no doubt, the employment offices will be examining candidates for industry.

Meanwhile, here we sit, reflectively spitting out our watermelon pips . . .

18 The sacristan

Keep your mouth shut, close your eyes and ears, and you will never have any trouble. But open your mouth, or become inquisitive, and you will have trouble all your life.

— LAO TZU

SATURDAY, 15 OCTOBER

Back to Canton. Just time to take a shower before Mr Hou snatches us away to take us to a magnificent restaurant, full to bursting with Chinese families treating themselves to a big blowout. In a private dining-room jutting out over the river, some dignitaries are awaiting us. It is the official banquet given by the Canton Cultural Association. Around the table are the vice-president of the Association, a former officer of the Eighth Route Army who is now principal of a large teachers' college; a very young woman who heads the Textile Workers' Union; a journalist, a judge of the municipal court, two professors of psychology from the teachers' college, the young beauty in the green polka-dot dress, a freshly-shaved Mr Hou, and a smirking Pi.

The menu exceeds anything we have seen up to now. There are thirty dishes at the very least: shrimps with nuts, meat stuffed with olives, preserved eggs, chicken with bamboo shoots, deep-fried pork, whole fish, pork in sweet sauce, roast duck, soup made from the flesh of three snakes, and an infinite number of pastries; the whole washed down with wine and bamboo alcohol. Is that all? No. We munch on lotus-flower birds with exquisite flesh. Then we start again with chicken, fish-stomachs, and pork, prepared in a still more ingenious manner. The feast concludes with a fish soup.

Starting stiffly, the speeches and toasts get warmer and warmer. For the hundredth time, Trudeau performs his number: 'China and Canada, joined — *jiga* — by an ocean felicitously named Pacific', and Hébert gives his regular toast in Chinese, without so much as glancing at his notes. In short, perfect euphoria reigns. Never have Canadians and Chinese said so many amiable things to each other in so short a time.

SUNDAY, 16 OCTOBER

Mr Hou had not foreseen that we would want to go to mass this morning. When we mention it to him, he gives a little frown, but assures us that he finds our request perfectly legitimate. It's agreed. Pi will go with us.

There are about forty of the faithful, and among them we notice a few young people, and some family groups. There is no sermon. After mass we head for the sacristy to greet the priest, a man in his sixties. Pi, who was waiting for us at the door with the polka-dot girl, runs up, visibly alarmed. 'Where are you going like that?' he asks.

'To shake the priest's hand — '

'But — but — '

'To have a little chat with him.'

'One moment, I'll go and find out if he can see you.'

Pi comes back after two minutes. 'Unfortunately the priest who speaks French is out of town.'

'That's all right. We'll say hullo — in Latin if necessary — to the one who just said mass.'

'No, really, he's very busy, he can't see you.' Pi is dancing about — he takes our arms to drag us out of the church. Just a moment, young man!

We are still parleying when the priest, who has understood exactly what was going on, comes to meet us. A magnificent head, with gentle, deepset eyes. How we would like to talk at leisure with this man. But that is clearly not on the program; to insist would land him squarely in a delicate situation vis-à-vis the authorities. We content ourselves with shaking his hand and saying a few unimportant words. *He speaks impeccable French.*

For the first time since we have been in China, there is no question of 'having a little tea'.

In Mr Hou's absence, Pi decides that he will have to make the best of this unforeseen incident. He introduces to us a pale

young man whom he has unearthed in the sacristy: 'The secretary of the Catholic parish association.' It is clear that with
this unusual sacristan present we can go ahead. 'He will answer
all your questions.'

Well, let's see. The conversation is taking place in the street,
in front of the church door. We bombard the 'answerable' one
with questions. Passersby gather round us, all the more interested
since our remarks are ironical to say the least. Pi loses his head;
he doesn't know which way to turn. The crowd grows. 'Come
on,' says Pi, furious, 'the secretary will go to the hotel with us.
It'll be a better place for discussion.' Why not?

We get the strong impression that the secretary is the man
imposed by the party on the parish to steer the study groups
in the 'right' direction, and to make brief reports, not to the
priest, but to the government. At all events, he seems poorly
grounded in religious questions, contenting himself with vague,
stammering answers and contradicting himself without turning
a hair. Furthermore, he has been in Canton for only ten years.
(It's noticeable, by the way, that most of the 'cadres' we have
met in Canton come from other regions, and they don't even
speak Cantonese. Can it be that there is less enthusiasm here?)
When we ask the 'sacristan' if there are still seminaries in
Canton, he answers that Cantonese seminarists go to Shanghai.
We know, of course, that there are no seminaries there. Nothing
embarrasses him, though, and he contradicts the evidence with
disarming innocence. As was to be expected, he gives us the
party line on foreign missionaries — 'spies in the pay of the
capitalists' and 'Chiang's men'. Clearly we are dealing with an
impostor, and we let him see that we know it. Pi is simply
beside himself throughout the interview. Innocently, we ask him
questions about the state of his soul.

Of course there is no doubt at all that many foreign missionaries believed that the fate of the Catholic Church was bound up
with that of the Kuomintang. In Formosa many of them are still
preparing themselves to return to China in the wake of Chiang
Kai-shek's armies. This astonishing attitude suggests that some
of them, in all good faith, took sides politically when they were
in China.

We are not naive enough to believe that the Church would have been tolerated by the régime for long, even if it had never made a mistake. All the same, wouldn't the Christians have resisted Communist seduction more vigorously if the missionaries had not supplied ready arguments for anti-Catholic propaganda? Would the Chinese Church have been transformed so quickly into a national church, separated from Rome, if the missionaries had relied less on the protection of foreign powers whose presence in China, which was anything but a Christian presence, constituted an offence against *all* Chinese? If the missionaries had lived in greater poverty — closer, that is, to the hungry people to whom they were teaching the Gospel of the Poor? Finally, if the hierarchy had become Chinese sooner than it did?

Because of a few errors, it was possible to ruin the reputation of all missionaries very quickly, to the point where relatively few Chinese Catholics could be found to defend them.

Once the missionaries were either expelled from China or imprisoned, the hierarchy found itself partly decapitated. It was easy then to attack the Pope as being under the tutelage of the imperialists. Next, the laity and lower clergy were set in opposition to the Chinese bishops under the pretext of 'democratizing the Church'. This sapping operation was helped by the Marxist experts who infiltrated into the 'patriotic study groups' imposed on all Catholic parishes. In discussions with often ill-prepared Christians, the Marxists had it all their own way.

The Chinese constitution guarantees freedom of religion, but the terribly effective methods used by the State to destroy the Catholic Church make this guarantee totally meaningless. A young Chinese is free to go to mass. But if he does, how can he pass the examination in Marxism that will determine his admission to university, his promotion, or his increase in salary?

Whatever our hosts may say, a Catholic in the New China cannot be anything but a pariah.

At the hotel we are told that a gentleman has left a message for us — it's McIntosh, who wasn't supposed to be coming to Canton. It is with the greatest pleasure that we rediscover this man of sound judgements and delightful humour. He tells us about a few of his latest discoveries, including a snake-market.

After a glorious feast, in which McIntosh proves himself a remarkable gastronome, we shake hands warmly: he to disappear into Kwantung, we to leave this very night for Peking and, soon afterwards, Canada. So farewell, dear old McIntosh!

MONDAY, 17 OCTOBER

Canton to Peking, via Wuhan. Nearly two days and two nights on the train — a mere trifle of 1500 miles.

In the dining-car, rather than sample the 'European' cuisine, Trudeau shares a table with Hou and Pi, and treats himself to sea-slugs, fish stomachs, and preserve of goose. Our Leader seems to have some matter he wants to get off his chest. Could it be something about the polka-dot girl?

From a distance the discussion appears to be charged with emotion. But, later, Trudeau contents himself with remarking laconically: 'Chinese Marxists are like Quebec collegians. On questions of religion and sex, they lose their sang-froid.'

There follow some reflections on the mistrust the Marxists feel for foreign visitors. But the examples Trudeau gives are not the ones we were expecting. He recalls the incident at the Commune of the Flowery Mountain, when the director claimed not to know the purpose of the four enormous antennae erected on the edge of his commune. And the curt reply of our guide the time we asked him what road we were travelling on: 'That is not important for you to know.' Similarly the attitude of another one, who no matter how wide he opened his eyes couldn't manage to see a pylon standing on the horizon, which had excited our curiosity. Finally the rebuff Micheline Legendre met when she asked permission to photograph some ordinary meteorological instruments at the Shanghai industrial fair.

These are small points that take nothing away from the hospitality with which we have been overwhelmed. Still, they show how deeply rooted in the subconscious (and how naively expressed) is the secret distrust of the young revolutionaries for the powerful enemy we represent.

Peking in the afternoon. The time of our departure is near, and we drag Pi and Mr Hou through the shops. We go past the celebrated Peking Hotel, a confusing mixture of large buildings piled on each other. During the two tourist seasons, centred on the First of October and May Day, nearly a thousand guests are put up here, chosen from the most important delegations, according to the distinction of the delegates or the political importance of the countries they represent; *we* don't stay at the Peking Hotel! Outside these two seasons, the haughty palace is as dead as a hotel at Percé in January. This is only October the eighteenth, and it is empty, as forlorn as a ship abandoned at sea.

19 Sightseeing in the last few days

The heart of the sage, like a mirror, should reflect every object but be sullied by none. — CONFUCIUS

WEDNESDAY, 19 OCTOBER

Three sunny and beneficent hours in the gardens of the Summer Palace, where the imperial families of the Manchu Dynasty used to come and rest from the hubbub of Peking.

The travellers go into raptures over these elaborate palaces, temples, and pavilions, rising out of the verdure around the Kunming Lake. A pretty scene; but several details make us feel rather uncomfortable — such as the restoration of the murals, achieved no doubt in record time by artistic shock-troops within the framework of the Great Leap Forward. Of course it was necessary to renovate these murals, damaged by time and — as Mr Hou doesn't fail to point out to us — 'by the French and English imperialist invaders of 1860 and the Kuomintang bandits'. But why entrust this delicate task to daubers whose only qualification must have been to have got first-class honours in the political examination?

This 500-acre garden contains the best and the worst: admirable landscapes, and congested pavilions where one finds, jumbled up together, fine old prints, Chang statuettes, and a portrait of the Empress Tz'u Hsi by a French painter whose technique would be bound to please Chinese fans of 'socialist realism'. This empress is said to have squandered a loan intended for the construction of a navy by building instead various useless and costly horrors like the famous marble boat that is forever moored at the edge of the lake. Which was at least an original means to pave the way for revolution.

But we are quibbling. On the whole, our tour of the Summer Palace will remain one of our happy memories of China, if only

for its banks of flowers, its smiling strollers, and its goldfish —
which stare at us with their great protruding eyes from the
depths of their terra-cotta prison, hopelessly flapping their in-
credibly long translucent fins.

The afternoon is given to shopping expeditions. We are
leaving the day after tomorrow, and Mr Hou understands that
we want to take back to Canada a few prints and a few yards of
brocade.

We go all over a big five-storey department store, which would
be comparable to our own establishments of the same kind if
the lighting were better and the décor more sophisticated. But
why, in a poor country, would a State-owned shop press its
customers to buy? Not without astonishment, we note that this
and all other shops, down to the smallest boutiques in Peking,
offer a considerable range of merchandise. They are filled to
bursting with men and women briskly buying such unnecessary
things as little nylon animals, cigarette boxes of lacquered wood,
embroideries, and artificial flowers.

Hébert wants to buy a Chinese violin, and a clerk shows him
two. He chooses the cheaper, which still costs three dollars. At
once a small Red Army soldier buys the other one, for six
dollars.

The counters where 'cult objects' are sold are especially well
patronized: red flags, photographs of Chairman Mao, silk
squares with Chou En-lai's picture, handkerchiefs with patriotic
slogans, and so on.

In the dress department we search in vain for the blue cotton
uniform that all Chinese women used to wear in the early years
of the régime. More and more they are coming back to the *chi-
pao*, that lovely adjustable Chinese dress, with no décolletage
but slit at the thigh.

THURSDAY, 20 OCTOBER

Today, at last, we are to see the Great Wall.

Leaving Peking early in the morning, we drive for a few
hours before we reach a series of walls, crossing the valley and
climbing the mountains. They take our breath away; clearly

they were built by genies. 'But this isn't the Wall,' says Mr Hou, smiling at our astonishment. 'These are just customs barriers.'

We keep on until we perceive a gigantic tower blocking the way. On either side of it, the Wall crosses the valley and thrusts into the mountains, running along the crests as far as the eye can see.

Penetrating more than two thousand miles into the interior of China, the Wall is one of the wonders of the world, and incontestably one of the most extraordinary things we have seen in all our travels. Its height varies from twenty to thirty feet, its thickness from sixteen to twenty-five. It has been called the longest cemetery in the world, because of the innumerable labourers who were worn out during its building. Astonomers have calculated that of all the works of Man, the Wall is the only one that would be visible from Mars. It is something that passes all understanding.

We climb nimbly up inside the tower and walk out along the Wall a good third of a mile towards the peaks. Sometimes it is so steep that the Wall is transformed into a gigantic staircase. At intervals there is a canal to carry the water off; in other places, steps going down the inner side. By these the garrison climbed up when the advanced posts signalled the approach of an enemy. When the danger was past, the soldiers went down again to cultivate the soil.

This is our second-last day in China, but we feel that today we have found one of the keys to the Chinese mystery. The reader may remember that from the day after our arrival we were struck by the force of numbers, which is so obvious wherever you look in China. But it's not enough for a country to have the largest labour force in the world; it must also know how to organize it. And that is just what many Western observers doubt — that China is capable of organizing itself into an industrial power.

Surely they are deceiving themselves. The Grand Canal that still unites China from north to south, and this Great Wall that crosses the country from east to west, are permanent evidence of an organizing genius that has never been equalled, even by the pyramid-builders. And they go back to an era when our ancestors, hungry and dressed in the skins of beasts, were still fleeing into the forests of Europe.

It is true that for some centuries the feudal system, in collaboration with Western capitalism, found it profitable to keep the people in a state of disorganization and stupefaction. The feudal lords had the power, the Westerners the profits, and the people the misery; it is not surprising that China was declared incapable of the smallest industrial development.

But here is a régime that shows the Westerners to the door and the feudal lords to the gallows; ten years later, China is already proving that it can become the leading industrial power in the world. This country is still eighty-five per cent rural; but that already gives it more industrial workers than Britain, with a population that is eighty per cent urban. Naturally China is still far from possessing the industrial equipment of countries that began their industrial revolutions fifty or a hundred years ago. But already the industrial fairs of Shanghai and Canton offer foreign buyers an extraordinarily wide range of products, from ingenious toys and sporting goods to heavy equipment and electronic apparatus.

True, we have seen only *one* steel complex, *one* automotive works, *one* sleeping-car factory, and so on. And skeptics may well tell us that these are false fronts, or even exceptional successes by which we shouldn't be overimpressed. That is not our opinion; if you can make one factory work, you can make a thousand, given time, education, and organization. Now, as for time, it is on the side of China, whose rate of growth exceeds ours. As for education, we have said enough in other chapters to underline the importance the Chinese attach to it. And as for organizing talent, they have it to burn.

Until the entire country is organized, technique manifests itself in the most diverse examples. On the First of October, for instance, the organization of the parade, the movement of the crowds, and the transport of a few thousand guests of honour were done with clockwork precision. Similarly the crossing of the Yangtze, on ferries that took on some railway cars while disembarking others, ran with a smoothness that would astound the English or the Scandinavians, who are familiar with this kind of operation. Finally construction techniques whereby blast-furnaces are finished in four months and gigantic buildings in ten are certainly the result of remarkable co-ordination of materials and manpower.

The Chinese a disorganized and technically deprived creature? It is a legend invented by the Westerner to ease his conscience for relegating this nation to the status of coolies.

On the way back we visit the tombs of the Mings, the most recent of them built four hundred years ago. We inspect that of the Emperor Yung Lo, who died in 1424. But what impresses the visitor most is the avenue leading to the tombs. In the middle of a bare plateau, it traces a long curve that seems to be going into eternity. On either side of this avenue are thirty-six statues, five to twelve feet high: two standing elephants, two crouching elephants, camels, lions, horses, dragons, dogs, and, to lead this unlikely caravan, a few human beings, officers and high officials, face to face, staring at each other through the ages.

In the evening the farewell banquet. The time has come at last for thanks and farewell speeches. Our Leader nearly ruins everything as he launches in his turn into a Chinese toast. He proposes that we drink to Universal Peace (*taiping*) but, seriously handicapped by the generous flow of liquid hospitality, he has the misfortune to pronounce this word like the capital of Formosa (Taipei).

There is consternation on all the Chinese faces. Our hosts are agitated, Trudeau persists and gets himself in deeper. The affair concludes in indescribable uproar.

FRIDAY, 21 OCTOBER

At four o'clock (it's still night, for heaven's sake!) Mr Hou invades our rooms, followed by Pi and some porters. 'We must hurry,' says Mr Hou, with the anxious air of a captain who is expecting mutiny.

'But the plane doesn't go till eight —'

'Exactly. A plane doesn't wait.'

To save still more time, he has had breakfast brought to our rooms.

We reach the airport at least two hours ahead of departure time. There is a delegation from the Cultural Association, led by the vice-president, Mr Wen. We pretend not to notice the huge bunches of flowers that will be presented to each of us shortly, just before take-off. The weather is magnificent, with a fine blue sky into which a sparkling Tupolev will fly at any moment.

Eight o'clock. Mr Hou gives us his last advice, Pi translates Mr Wen's last friendly remarks . . .

Eight-thirty. We have been accustomed to greater punctuality in the New China.

Nine o'clock. Soviet pilots have a reputation for over-caution. No doubt they are checking one last bolt.

Nine-thirty. We venture to ask Mr Wen a timid question about take-off time. 'It is snowing at Irkutsk. Our aircraft never take off when it is snowing at Irkutsk.'

Eleven o'clock. Every time the loudspeakers start to crackle, we press Pi into service. 'It's nothing; a lady has lost her umbrella.' It is still snowing at Irkutsk.

Noon. 'Supposing we eat,' says Mr Wen. He too has been on his feet since four.

One o'clock. 'It is snowing at Irkutsk.'

Finally the loudspeakers announce that snow is still falling at Irkutsk and departure is postponed until tomorrow morning. While an airport employee throws the bouquets of faded flowers into a basket, we go back to the hotel.

SATURDAY, 22 OCTOBER

Starting out again, this foggy morning, we instinctively recall the first impressions that struck us that sunny Sunday of our arrival.

This is the classic road of Asia, we thought then: where you meet innumerable pedestrians, moving slowly under the torrid sun; plenty of mule-carts, bicycles, a few buses discharging eternal travellers; rare automobiles, blowing their horns incessantly, and constantly going out of gear to save fuel. And we were impatient to discover where this road led.

We knew it now, after five weeks in China. We knew that this road free of refuse, these pedestrians without rags, were not exceptional: in all our travels, even the unplanned ones, and in the poorest quarters, we had never met a beggar or seen the stinking filth that is characteristic of nearly every road in Asia. We knew that those innumerable little trees that covered the neighbouring fields were not there to impress the new arrival; they were part of a plan of afforestation that was little by little wresting the Gobi Desert from the domination of the sands, a plan whose traces we saw among the barest mountains, and right up to the foot of the Great Wall. We knew that those dormitory buildings rising on the approaches to Peking were duplicated in incalculable numbers in all the suburbs of all the industrial cities of China.

And on this morning of our departure, at the hour when the workers are on their way to the factory, as we watch thousands of cyclists looming up out of the chilly fog, we know that they are no longer travelling on 'the classic road of Asia'. They are travelling the road of the future, a future so filled with promise and with trials that even the most audacious planners cannot trace its outline.

Eight-thirty. Half an hour late. So what? It's perfectly normal.

Nine o'clock. 'There is fog at Irkutsk.' *No*!

Ten o'clock. Resigned, we wander through the vast airport, trying to comfort some seething South Americans who are calling down curses on Irkutsk and all Siberia.

Eleven o'clock. At last the fog has lifted from that unlucky town. Our departure is announced. But first come some touching farewells: how could one fail to become attached to so worthy a man as Mr Hou, or to his echo, the devoted Pi?

After five short weeks and five thousand miles of adventures, of factories, and of McIntosh, we leave the New China, our arms loaded with fresh flowers.

Innocents as before.

Epilogue

We announced in the Preamble our intention of correcting the notion of the Yellow Peril. That is what we have done. The reader will have grasped one point, that the Asiatic tidal wave is not going to engulf the earth tomorrow.

First, China will have to engulf its own country. For at present ninety-four per cent of its population is concentrated in two-fifths of its area. And China has realized that to lay a solid foundation for its industrial development it must begin by improving its own soil. That is, it must prospect, take stock of, and colonize immense semi-desert regions, set up communications, build roads and railways; it must found cities and make industries spring up where for five thousand years only caravans have been.

So the real threat is not the Yellow Peril of our nightmares; it is the eventual threat of economic rivalry in the markets of the world, and the nearer threat of an ideological success that is already enabling China to help — with its capital, its technicians, and above all its example — the even poorer countries of Asia, Africa, and Latin America.

We have said little in this book about international politics, because little was said to us in China on the subject. The government of Mao Tse-tung seems to take the attitude that it needs the world no more than the world needs it. It knows that *in fact* the problems of peace and war, disarmament, and nuclear peril cannot be settled without taking into account a State that represents a quarter of the human race. It knows that the question of its admission to the United Nations will be settled eventually, and that when the time comes the United States will lose more face than if it had acted without being compelled to. In 1951 the United States resolution against China received seventy-one per cent of the votes at the United Nations; in 1960 a similar resolution received no more than forty-three per cent, and abstentions had increased from eight to twenty-two per cent.

Time is on its side, and China is in no hurry — except on one point: Taiwan. The occupation of this island by Mao Tse-tung's implacable and, so to speak, personal enemy constitutes an intolerable affront to the Communists. For twenty-five years the Kuomintang persecuted, hounded, and decimated the Communists in every corner of China. After the Communists' hard-won victory, was it to be borne that the Kuomintang should have the right to occupy, unhindered, an island recognized since the Cairo Conference by all the great powers (including China) as an integral part of China? Still more, were the armies of Chiang Kai-shek to gather strength there, to prepare an invasion with impunity?

The Communist Party regards Taiwan as a matter of honour. And it has seen to it that patriotic emotion on this subject is pushed to its highest pitch from one side of China to the other. We ourselves have seen the evidence of this campaign in the museums, at the ballet, in speeches, on posters, in the schools, at the theatre, and in the newspapers. In a public movie-theatre we saw a short documentary in which young people were being trained in war games. Watching this film, and hearing the name 'Taiwan' coming in over and over again, we had the horrible feeling that we were witnessing a repetition (minus uniforms) of the thirties in the Europe of the dictatorships.

However, there is one fact that tends to allay our fears: China is historically more an 'aggressed' than an aggressor nation. It has generally been the one to be invaded — forty times in the last century and a quarter! (And that is possibly the most impressive statistic to be found anywhere in this short book.)

But the epilogue is no place to settle a question like that. Let us simply add that the 'two-China' policy is based on profound ignorance of the Chinese mentality. The accredited anti-Communists, of course, will go on believing for the next fifty years that the Chinese are on the verge of rising against their Communist government, just as some people have believed the same thing of the USSR for forty-four years. But the American government and its allies are well aware that their Formosan policy is now based only on a question of prestige. In fact, since the United States commissioned its Polaris submarines, Taiwan has pretty well lost the military importance it had in 1950, when it was described as the world's biggest aircraft carrier.

Unhappily the obliteration of the human race has become a possibility to be reckoned with henceforth in all our calculations. And, in their innocence, the authors of the present volume cannot bring themselves to believe that a question of prestige is worth the trouble of setting off the final thermonuclear holocaust. This does seem like the judgement of innocents, to those 'informed' people who take nihilism, cynical or spiritual, for expert opinion.

It is true that, if the authors of *Two Innocents in Red China* are guilty of anything, it is naiveté. We had the naiveté to believe that what we saw with our own eyes did exist; and the further naiveté to think our readers capable of making the necessary adjustments in the often outrageous claims made by our Chinese informants. That is why we didn't always think it essential to interpose our critical judgement between the reader and the Chinese official we were quoting verbatim.

Readers conscientious enough to read epilogues deserve some reward. They will be the only ones to know of the final surprise McIntosh had in store for us.

Several days after the dispersal of the Canadian group, about 29 October, Trudeau was travelling from Leningrad to Paris when a storm forced his plane to land at Copenhagen. Just before it took off again, he ran into a group of travellers from Moscow to London who had had to take refuge at the same airport. So it was that, by an improbable coincidence, he perceived the cheerful face of McIntosh, in the act of lighting a cigar.

'Greetings, old McIntosh!'

He took a moment to recover from his surprise. Then he told how a snowstorm had kept his plane grounded for two days at Omsk, in Siberia. He had had to sleep in a primitive dormitory, and his poor tortoises had nearly perished of cold.

But the plane for Paris was ready to take off. A handshake, and Trudeau had to run for it, with a very 'British' voice calling after him, 'You know, my name isn't McIntosh. It's —'

A sound that might have been 'Hinton' was drowned out in the roar of the aircraft.